The Workplace Guide
to Time Management

The Workplace Guide to
TIME
MANAGEMENT

Best Practices to Maximize Productivity

Phoebe Gavin

**ROCKRIDGE
PRESS**

For general information on our other products and services or to obtain technical support, please contact our Customer Care Department within the United States at (866) 744-2665, or outside the United States at (510) 253-0500.

Rockridge Press publishes its books in a variety of electronic and print formats. Some content that appears in print may not be available in electronic books, and vice versa.

Interior and Cover Designer: Jami Spittler
Art Producer: Sue Bischofberger
Editor: Carolyn Abate
Production Editor: Mia Moran

Pattern used under license from iStockphoto.com

Author photo courtesy of Victoria Fleischer

ISBN: Print 978-1-64876-014-3 | eBook 978-1-64876-015-0

R0

TO YOU

Your potential is beyond
what you ever imagined.

Harness it.
Bring it into this world.

Contents

Introduction

How much can you accomplish in 24 hours?
We all have the same amount of time, but some people
use theirs for a bigger impact. It's not that they get more
done. It's that they get the right things done. This is the
essence of time management: doing the right things at
the right time. Time management is what makes success
possible, no matter where you work or who you work
for—a business, a not-for-profit organization, or yourself.
You can have the best ideas, the best products, or the best
services, but without time management, your operation will
limp to the finish line—if it gets there at all.

If you become that person who can internalize habits
and reflexes to keep yourself organized, prioritized, and
distraction-free, that's far beyond simply "good time management." That's when you become a master of your time.
Embrace the principles of a "Time Master" and you'll smash
efficiency and productivity together to ultimately drive stun-
ning results for your company and yourself. In this book,
we'll explore scientifically supported methods for improving
your time management skills so you can become a true
Time Master. Building these skills will keep you organized,
help you meet deadlines, improve your focus, and give you
space to enjoy your job. Strong time management skills

empower you to drive the results you want, build your professional reputation, and grow in your career.

Most importantly, time management creates calm. This transformative aspect of time management is why I care so much about it. I grew up with ADHD, and my lack of time management skills caused me to struggle from elementary school all the way through college. It showed in my grades, but more than that, it showed in my mental health. Medication helped me focus, but I had a hard time focusing on the right things. My repeat failures kept me in a perpetual state of anxiety, regret, and disappointment.

As I entered professional life, I hit a breaking point. After a scathing performance review at my first job, I felt like my reputation was damaged beyond repair. I quit a few weeks later. I didn't want my trouble with procrastination and prioritization to destroy any hope of a thriving career. I knew I needed to develop the skills and techniques to manage my time better.

While I looked for another job, I read everything I could about the psychology of time management. I was shocked to learn how bad the human brain is at making short-term decisions that offer long-term benefit. My poor time management was natural. I wasn't broken. My brain was doing precisely what it was designed to do. But I could train it to do better. By implementing the changes and the techniques in this book, I mastered my time and built a successful career. I don't even need ADHD medication anymore.

Now, as a life and career coach, I teach people how to spend their time on what's important. I help them learn how to avoid wasting time on things that don't matter—the things that don't move them forward. And I can help you, too—whether you are working your first job, putting in hours as a mid-level manager, or helming a big company as CEO. It makes no difference if you freelance from home or work a 40-hour office job. Every job requires good time management skills. As a bonus, you'll find that your personal life will benefit from learning to master your time.

I've assembled my best techniques in this book in hopes of saving you the time I spent trudging through the swamp of trial and error. If I can become a Time Master, you can, too.

How to Use This Book

You are about to transform the way you manage your time. Think of this book as taking you on a journey: one that begins with productivity struggles and ends with time mastery. I recommend keeping a journal as you read this book. There will be activities and exercises to help you gain clarity, brainstorm ideas, and solve problems. Don't just read the exercises. Do them in your journal, and use the results as a resource and for reference.

Each chapter starts with a story based on one of my real productivity coaching clients. The purpose of these stories is twofold. First, to remind you that you are not alone. Many people—with distinctive jobs, personalities, and demands—struggle with time management. They aren't stupid, broken, or undisciplined. They just need to grow in the skill. Second, these stories remind you that change is possible. Each of these clients went on to drastically improve their time management and succeed professionally. You can, too.

In chapter one, we'll take a hard look at where you are and how you currently manage your time. We'll identify what's not working and the root causes of your biggest time management challenges. We'll also reflect on the importance of breaking bad habits and envision what your life could look like if you had an effective productivity system.

In chapter two, we'll work through the most common obstacles to productivity: distracting work environments and technology. We'll identify some of the productivity traps that come with office environments and working from home. We'll also look at how technology holds us back from spending our time wisely. I'll help you create a system that turns your devices from enemies into allies.

In chapter three, we'll examine goals. We'll explore how to avoid goals that set you up for failure and learn how to design goals that actually work. We'll deal directly with how to set priorities that stick and how to develop your resistance to distraction.

In chapter four, we'll discuss what to do when things go wrong. We'll explore how to prevent setbacks and what to do when plans go awry. We'll also work through what to do when disaster strikes.

In the final chapter, we'll put it all together into a plan you can use to take your first steps in transforming your productivity habits. You'll be able to revisit the plan development process whenever you're ready to take the next step in your journey.

It's difficult to overstate how much of a positive impact effective time management can have on your life. I've seen it firsthand in my coaching clients. Once you've finished this book, you will have gained an incredibly valuable skill set. You'll be able to maximize your productivity in service of your most important goals. You'll reduce the stress and anxiety you feel at work. You'll finally be able to harness your most precious resource: time.

ONE

"I'll Get to It First Thing Tomorrow"

In this chapter, I lay the groundwork for a successful time management system. I start by exploring the most common causes and effects of poor time management. No two people have the same demands or challenges, so we'll also examine your situation's specific characteristics.

You may be excited to jump in and make changes, but don't skip this step. It's important to understand your "why" before your "how." I've had clients rush through it or insist on skipping it altogether. Without exception, they fail to get to the bottom of their problems. This leaves them unable to design a time management approach that works.

It's hard to create an effective solution for a problem you haven't fully identified. The clearer you are about your starting place, the better you'll be at building a time management system that works for you.

"Missing the Mark on Monday"

Chelsea is well-liked by her manager, Greg, and her teammates, but she drops the ball a little too often. She loses track of time, is late to meetings, and misses deadlines. Not by much, but often enough that she's developed a reputation for being a lovable space cadet. Her supervisor is done letting it slide, and this year's performance review shows it.

"At the end of the day," Greg says, "the team depends on you to do your part well and on time. The client's milestones are not negotiable. We can't move forward on the rest of the project until we have your deliverable in hand. When you miss your deadlines, you put the rest of the team in a time crunch to catch up and meet the client's milestones anyway. Your poor time management is a liability for the team."

Oof.

Greg continues through the brutal review, digging into each bullet in the "Areas for Development" section. Chelsea is prone to turning in presentation decks with typos. She forgets to complete a task assigned to her. She's late for meetings or sometimes misses them altogether. She takes on too much and then comes back later, apologizing for not having time to follow through.

All of it comes back to not being able to manage her time properly.

Greg puts down the performance review form and slides it across the table to Chelsea. "You're talented, Chelsea. You have great instincts. Great energy. Great ideas. But our clients aren't paying for great ideas. They're paying for great execution. You need to find a way to consistently get your work done on deadline and right the first time. If you aren't able to do that, we're going to have to escalate this beyond the two of us. I really don't want to do that."

Chelsea knows exactly what he means: some tough conversations with human resources.

As Greg outlines the administrative next steps for the review, Chelsea zones out. The list of performance problems seems overwhelming.

She doesn't want to be a liability for the team, and she certainly doesn't want to get fired. Chelsea loves her software development job and dreams of growing in the company, which has a strong track record of promoting from within. How is she going to get a promotion if she keeps letting everyone down? Anxiety rises in her chest, and she takes a deep breath so as not to become visibly upset.

Greg stands, frowning. Chelsea joins him and extends her hand for a shake. She summons all the determination she can and looks him in the eye, "Thank you for the feedback, Greg. I am going to fix this."

He nods curtly and leaves the room.

"I am going to fix this."

The Struggle Is Real

Time management in the office is a struggle for most of us because the typical office is full of distraction traps—it's rife with interruptions, unrealistic workloads, and random intrusions. For many of us, it goes something like the following scenario.

The report is due in your manager's inbox by 5 p.m. It's a behemoth, so you get to the office an hour early. Now you can make progress before the office explodes with activity. Except your phone won't stop dinging, and it's not even 9 a.m.

Every new email piles on a new task. Karen tells you a story every time she walks past your desk. You have three meetings today, and none pertain to you. Alan's birthday party is happening in the conference room next door. How are you supposed to be productive and efficient with all this chaos?

You do your best to deal with the interruptions. You check each notification. You respond to every email. You listen to Karen's third story because you don't want to be rude. You dutifully attend the pointless meetings. You try to ignore the birthday party.

Between your daily responsibilities and the barrage of disruptions, you've barely put a dent in the report, and panic creeps in. People are leaving the conference room and the noise subsides. Finally, some time to get things done. But it's . . . already 4 o'clock?!

You squeeze your eyes shut, rub your temples, and get up to head for the coffee pot. "I guess I'm in for another late night."

Identifying the Root of the Problem

The office should be where you do your best work. But for most people, the opposite is true. Instead, it's a productivity battlefield where you fight desperately to get something—anything—done before the end of the day. When the clock hits 5 p.m., many of us can't point to what we accomplished.

Why? The myriad disruptions that crash through our focus, hijack our priorities, and trample our plans. It's no wonder so many people struggle.

Everyone faces these sorts of problems at work. I see this all the time in my coaching practice. You are not alone. Yet the most successful among us find a way to consistently get things done. What gives? Not getting things done is a common symptom of a common problem: ineffective time management.

But it doesn't have to be like this. You can craft solutions that work for you once you look below the surface and find the root cause.

While it may seem like an overwhelming task, the rewards are worth the effort. When you manage your time effectively, you supercharge productivity and decrease stress. But most importantly, you won't waste time. Instead, you'll be investing time in the most exciting, impactful, and important aspects of your job.

So where do you start diagnosing your time management issues and start working toward becoming a Time Master? Let's explore.

How do you keep track of your tasks?
Time Masters have an airtight system for capturing incoming requests. They always know what is expected of them. Their colleagues can depend on them to remember tasks,

details, and deadlines. If you often forget what needs to be done and when, your task tracking system is broken. We'll explore ways to fix your tracking system in chapter two.

Are you overwhelmed by your workload?

Time Masters can accurately assess how long a task will take and if they have room for it. They know when to ask for additional context from their colleagues or supervisor. They also know how to say "no" or "not now" if a task simply doesn't fit at the time. If you have trouble with this, your task assessment system is broken. You may also need to develop your communication skills. In chapter two, I'll discuss ways to improve your communication.

Time Masters are continually assessing and reassessing how important tasks are. As new requests come in, they quickly identify where each should fit in the workday or workweek. They always work on the most important things first. They make sure they proactively communicate with their colleagues about when to expect completed tasks. If you have a hard time doing this, your prioritization system is broken. We'll explore ways to fix this in chapter three.

How much time do you lose to distractions?

Time Masters work hard to eliminate as many distractions as possible from their work environment. They realize some distractions are impossible to remove entirely, and they develop techniques that help them maintain focus. If you have a hard time doing this, your focus system is broken. In chapter three, we'll explore methods to boost your focus.

Do you have a hard time coping with external disruptions?

Time Masters still experience unexpected external disruptions. However, these interruptions don't get in the way of their productivity. They avoid rigid plans that can't withstand disruption. Instead, they anticipate disruptions and create flexible plans that can adjust. If you have a hard time doing this, your planning system is broken. We'll explore ways to fix it in chapter four.

Have you tried time management methods but given up because they didn't work?
There are many approaches to time management. Not all of them will suit your needs. Time Masters know the difference between a tactic that's a bad fit and one with potential that needs iteration or perseverance. They experiment with different approaches until they find a system that works. In chapter five, you'll learn how to construct the first iteration of your system, evaluate its effectiveness, and make adjustments.

The Usual Suspects

The modern world comes with all sorts of demands and distractions that keep us from staying on top of our most important priorities. Our brains were designed to find food, shelter, and community to stay alive, not to "manage time." To struggle with time management is to be human.

We have more demands than ever before. Trying to fit work, school, family, friends, and fun into 24 hours is impossible, but it's a task we all face. It's no wonder we so often find ourselves missing deadlines, failing to deliver the highest-quality work, or feeling drained beyond description.

In my years of coaching people, I've noticed patterns in the root causes of productivity issues. Whether these clients are new graduate students or seasoned executives, the same five mistakes are at the root of their time management problems. They look different for each person, but they are always there.

We overestimate how much time we have and underestimate how much time we need.

We each have so many urgent but disparate demands. Even with our best efforts, we struggle to accurately estimate how much time they will take. Sure, you have three hours of meetings today. But are you accounting for meeting prep, conversations running over, long goodbyes on the way back from the conference room, follow-up emails, and same-day deliverables you promised on the fly? Have you accidentally committed to seven hours of work when you only have five hours available?

We fail to set effective priorities.

With each day, we're greeted with an onslaught of meetings, messages, and people "just dropping by." With each interruption, something else is added to our to-do lists. It's easy to feel overwhelmed and to struggle with deciding which actions need attention. So we flit from task to task without making much progress on any of them. The day ends before we have accomplished anything.

We fail to use technology effectively.

Technology can help us stay organized, prioritized, and focused. But, more often than not, our devices distract and overwhelm us. Each ping signals a new email, text, phone call, or instant message. Our favorite websites and social media platforms are a few tantalizing clicks away. Our screens flood with notifications, and we can't help but tap-tap-tap so we don't miss anything "important" as time ticks by.

We let difficult emotions and bad habits get in the way.

We get used to our way of doing, feeling, and being. Even when we know certain habits and reflexes are uncomfortable or counterproductive, we cling to them. You might work long hours because you fear upsetting a supervisor, and then burn out. You might agree to an unrealistic deadline to impress a colleague, and then miss it. All that just to disappoint yourself and erode your professional reputation.

We fail to account for the fact that "life happens." There's an old military adage that's cribbed from a book by Prussian military commander Helmuth von Moltke: "No plan survives first contact with the enemy." It's true for civilians, too. In the past, you may have played a little too fast and loose with your time and then found yourself unprepared for an unexpected demand that was too urgent to ignore. Or you may have committed to a rigid timeline that made it impossible to find space for a new priority that was just as important.

My clients are often surprised at how much of an impact simple steps can make on their lives. Having clarity on where your time and energy should be focused each day creates a sense of calm, reduces procrastination, and makes life feel less overwhelming. Just think of what life would look like if you were able to dismantle these obstacles for good.

Areas for Improvement

You are reading this book for a reason.

Maybe you've noticed issues in your work performance you want to solve. Maybe Chelsea's story of missing deadlines and her lack of attention to detail in the beginning of this chapter rings a bell with you. Perhaps, like her, you've had a tough conversation with your boss about specific incidents or a pattern of problems in which little things start to add up into big things and suddenly your job or a promotion is at risk. Or maybe you're just being proactive about developing good habits. Either way, something brought you here.

My clients come to me from all walks of life, and I'm always inspired by how far they can go in their time management journeys. This transformation only happens if they start their journey with an honest view of their individual challenges and goals—which is your next task.

Identifying Pain Points

No matter what your time management challenges look like, it's critical to remember that you're not alone. Time management takes work—even for people who appear effortlessly productive. And the brain we're stuck with isn't designed to help us deal effectively with these issues.

Distractions

Distractions come for all of us. Your brain is wired to be distracted. Researchers from Princeton University and the University of California at Berkeley found that while the human brain is capable of long periods of intense focus, it automatically scatters moments of distraction throughout.

During these moments, we subconsciously reach out with our senses to see if something else is more important—like our unread email count. For our ancient ancestors, this brain activity helped them notice when a threat had infiltrated a moment of safety. But for the average accountant, this relic of caveman days could cost him his job.

Disparate Priorities

Juggling priorities is a reality for all of us. Dozens of demands are piled on each day. Tiny things like Jim interrupting you to ask how to set the printer to double-sided. Big things like your boss giving you a new high-profile assignment. Meaningless things like signing a birthday card for an employee you rarely work with. Impactful things like a kickoff meeting for that multimillion-dollar project.

All of these demands create a mental traffic jam, and your brain, which loves the instant gratification of the short-term win, does a terrible job of prioritizing what's actually important. This can snowball from being late to meetings or turning in work with typos to risking a client account, like with Chelsea and Greg in our story from the beginning of the chapter.

Unexpected Curveballs

Life happens to all of us. Just when we think we have the master plan designed, the internet goes down. Or the fire alarm goes off. Or there's a surprise visit from the CEO. Or little Allison needs to be picked up from school. The loss of time and momentum can make it seem impossible to recover from the day's curveballs.

If we're all faced with the same challenges, what is the difference between Time Masters and those who struggle? It's not that they have fewer distractions and demands. It's that Time Masters have better systems and habits for managing their time.

Tip: Writing It All Down

Take a moment to reflect. Grab a sheet of paper or a journal and reflect on your last week of work. How many of these were true for you?

- Interruptions from colleagues made it hard for me to focus.
- I forgot to do something I was expected to do.
- My calendar was packed with meetings or phone calls.
- I wasted time working on something that wasn't actually important.
- I was distracted by my phone or my favorite websites.
- I procrastinated on something I knew I needed to do.
- I was overwhelmed by how much work I had.
- I spent too much time checking work-related emails, texts, or instant messages.
- I made a little progress on several tasks but didn't complete any of them.
- I skipped lunch or worked late to get things done.
- I spent more time "putting out fires" than getting real work done.
- My personal life intruded on work time.
- I missed a deadline.
- I turned in work that was below the expected quality.
- A task took much longer than I expected.

Are there any other areas that aren't working? Anything else you want to improve? Add them to your list.

Use this list as a benchmark for your time management journey. As you implement new tactics and internalize new habits, these missteps should happen less frequently. Make a point of reviewing this list at the end of each week to see how you're doing.

Moment of Introspection

While this book will give you a clear, actionable plan for maximizing your time management, you will still have to do the work. Improving your productivity requires learning new habits and unlearning old ones. There will be times when it feels difficult. You'll hit rough patches and have setbacks. There will be times when you just don't feel like doing the work.

The difference between people who succeed and people who don't is simple: The successful ones have an understanding of their reasons for becoming the most productive version of themselves—their **Deep Why**. The **Deep Why** is the real desire behind the obvious reason for doing something. This powerful motivator helps you persevere when the journey gets challenging.

For example, Howard is a project manager at an architecture firm. His pattern of mistakes has his boss micromanaging him. The tension in that relationship is causing him to bring stress home. Howard's wife is frustrated with his behavior after work, and he feels guilty for being irritable.

He wants to get his boss off his back, but that's a Surface Why. The **Deep Why** is wanting to protect his relationship from spillover work stress. Whether your **Deep Why** is about your family life, like in Howard's case, or about salvaging your career, like in Chelsea's story from the beginning of the chapter, finding your **Deep Why** is key to fixing your time management issues.

EXERCISE:
Identifying Your Deep Whys

Grab your notes from the "Writing It All Down" activity and answer the following four questions:

Question 1: What is happening?
In the "Writing It All Down" activity, you outlined the time management challenges you're experiencing. These challenges are your What but not your Why. Review this list again.

Question 2: How is this impacting me?
How does your list of What make you feel? What are some of the consequences these challenges are causing at work? Are they affecting your personal life? These are your Surface Whys. You may find that multiple issues on your list feed into the same Surface Why.

Write down these Surface Whys in complete sentences that connect the problem to its direct result. For example: "When I miss a deadline, my supervisor gets on my case."

Question 3: Why do I want to improve this?
Examine your list of Surface Whys. How are they affecting you? Are they holding you back from being who you want to be? Are they negatively impacting your career? Do they change the way you see yourself? Do they change the way others see you? Are they creating a crisis in your life? These are The Stakes.

Write down The Stakes in complete sentences. For example: "When my supervisor gets on my case, it makes me anxious and stressed."

Question 4: What is the Deep Why?
Examine your list of Stakes. What would life be like if these never improved—or got worse? Why is it so essential to avoid that outcome? The answer to this question should connect to your core values, desires, and drives. If it doesn't, you may still be working with a Surface Why. Keep going deeper.

Express each Deep Why in a complete sentence in an I Want To/Because format. For example: "I want to resolve this anxiety because the stress I'm bringing home damages my relationship."

Weighing the Benefits

In the previous activity, you identified your personal motivations for wanting to fix your time management problems. Whatever is on your personal motivation list, there are five key advantages to properly managing your time that should also be on your list. These benefits apply no matter who you are, what business you're in, or where you are in your career. Take a moment to consider how much better your life can be when you manage your time well.

Time management improves your work product.
One of the hallmarks of poor time management is rushing to meet deadlines. Rushed work products are more likely to have errors, missed instructions, or forgotten elements. This work often has to be fixed or redone, which takes even more time away from your other priorities. When you manage your time correctly, you have enough time to complete your work well and not redo it.

Time management improves your professional reputation.

Mishaps at work rarely affect you alone. They ripple out-ward and impact your colleagues' ability to get their jobs done, too. When your colleagues have to pick up slack because of your time management failures, you develop a reputation for being unreliable. It's hard to progress pro-fessionally when your coworkers don't trust you. Proper time management allows you to be the best version of your professional self—the version people want to work with, promote, and pay top dollar.

Time management gives you more free time.

Distractions, procrastination, perfectionism, and multitask-ing are inefficiencies that make even the simplest tasks take too long. A sound time management system allows you to preserve that time—and save even more—for what matters most to you. You can use that time for the most impactful and enjoyable tasks or simply to have a better balance at work (no more skipped lunch breaks!).

Time management reduces your stress.

Every missed deadline or forgotten assignment creates stress, pressure, and worry. Effective time management prevents these failures and helps your entire work experi-ence run smoothly. This lack of friction improves your life in and out of the office. You feel more confident and calm when your professional to-do list is under control.

Time management frees you from regret.

Hindsight can be brutal for a person with poor time management. In the moment, it's hard to see what is sabotaging your productivity. But looking back, it's usually apparent where time was misspent. Regret soon follows. Regret is one of the most damaging human emotions because it anchors your thoughts to things you can't change. A reliable time management system allows you to focus on the present and the future instead of the past—even when things don't go exactly as planned.

Taking the First Step

You're ready to take the first step toward building your time management system. We'll start by thoroughly evaluating your current context. We'll explore how your off time impacts your work time. We'll examine your work environment and how that facilitates or impedes your productivity. Then we'll take a high-level look at how you structure your time at work. Lastly, we'll explore ways to put it all together without getting overwhelmed. I've seen so many clients use this sequence to take back their time, reduce their stress, and have a better work-life balance, and I know you can, too.

Your 24-Hour Schedule

"Give me six hours to chop down a tree and I will spend the first four sharpening the axe" is a quote often wrongly attributed to Abraham Lincoln. While he might not have said it, the principle is priceless: Proper preparation is essential to efficient execution.

Do you spend enough time "sharpening the axe"?

If you often fail to leave on time or forget things at home, consider getting everything ready the night before. It's a powerful act of axe-sharpening that takes as little as 15 minutes.

- ○ Check your calendar to identify the next day's needs.

- Collect any necessary materials, technology, or equipment.

- Set out your clothing.

- Prep a healthy breakfast.

- Make sure your alarm is set.

We've all had days where work felt like a slog because we were sick or tired, or had a personal problem weighing us down. At work, you draw on your physical, emotional, and mental resources to get things done. If those tanks are empty, you'll struggle to do quality work in a timely manner.

Time Masters know this and prioritize effective self-care. They keep the body tank full by consistently:

- Sleeping seven to nine hours

- Eating a balanced diet, including fruits and vegetables

- Moving their body every day in enjoyable ways

- Resting when they feel sick or fatigued

- Seeing a medical professional when they're experiencing persistent or severe issues

They keep the heart tank full by consistently:

- Spending time with fun, affirming people

- Contributing to causes or community organizations

- Maintaining emotionally grounding practices such as journaling, meditation, or prayer

- Reducing unnecessary stressors

○ Seeing a mental health professional when they're experiencing persistent or severe issues

They keep the mind tank full by consistently:

○ Engaging in activities that are novel or require problem-solving

○ Reading books, websites, or articles they enjoy

○ Playing games that challenge their brain

○ Maintaining fun hobbies that help them learn or practice skills

○ Allowing the mind time to wander, daydream, and be creative

When you're feeling pressed for time, self-care can feel like one thing you don't have time for. You may think it's too hard to maintain healthy habits. This is a mental trap. Of course, it's not possible to do everything every day. Start small and think in terms of weeks or months instead of days to steadily make your life happier, healthier, and more productive.

To learn more about how to build healthy, sustainable habits in your personal life, visit betterwithphoebe.com /bodyheartmind.

Your Physical Work Environment

How does your workspace make you feel? Are you comfortable? Companies design offices with various priorities, but these two rarely make the list. And at-home setups are often thrown together. The result is workspaces that are distracting, uncomfortable, and sometimes downright demoralizing. But there are ways to improve your workspace.

The best workspaces boost your mood, keep your energy up, and help you focus. The worst workspaces are draining and sometimes even physically painful.

If your workspace is draining your productivity, talk to your supervisor. Your company may be willing to make improvements. If that's not possible, consider making improvements yourself. Investments in improving your work environment, whether at home or in the office, are investments in the quality of your work. Consider these four characteristics of your work environment:

Workstation Ergonomics

Most workstations include your chair, desk, keyboard, monitor, and mouse. It may also include secondary equipment such as file storage, your telephone, or other items you use to work. The more often you use a piece of equipment, the more important it is to make sure it's in good working condition. The same can be said for comfortable, healthy posture. If you find you're slouching, for example, consider making some changes to help you sit up straight. This could be as simple as replacing a chair, adjusting a monitor, or putting a laptop on a riser.

Even the most ergonomic of workstations can cause problems if you don't move around. The human body is not designed to sit for eight hours a day. But so many of us do just that. You'll feel better, think more clearly, and have more energy if you stand up, stretch, and take walks—even just twice a day.

Sound

Some people say the sound of a bustling office makes them more productive, but science says otherwise. In a 2000 study published in the *Journal of Applied Psychology*, participants exposed to office noise solved fewer puzzles than participants working in silence. Another study published in 2003 in the *Journal of Environmental Psychology* found that workers in offices with less ambient noise reported less job stress than those in louder offices. If your work environment is loud, try headphones. Experiment with what you listen to, as some sounds distract more than others.

Light
Natural light has a strong positive effect on mood, energy, and productivity. If your workspace lacks natural light, try to re-create it. Dimmer, warmer light mimics sunset and makes the brain create sleep hormones, while brighter, cooler light mimics daylight and increases alertness.

Aesthetic
A workspace that reflects your personal style will make you happier than a blank canvas. Find ways to incorporate colors, patterns, and textures you enjoy into your workspace aesthetic. Add photos of your loved ones, art that inspires you, or fun decorative accents.

This may seem like a long list of changes, but resist the urge to overhaul your entire work environment at once. For budget-friendly, time-efficient tips on optimizing your workstation and adding movement to the workday, visit betterwithphoebe.com/myworkstation.

Your Psychological Work Environment

A positive psychological environment can set the stage for an efficient and fulfilling work experience. A challenging psychological environment fills work with distractions and slows us down. Many people think it's unprofessional to have emotions at work and ignore them while on the clock. But your ability to be productive is directly impacted by your emotional state. Emotions should be managed or leveraged, not suppressed or ignored.

What emotions do you usually experience at work? The following are the ones I see come up for my coaching clients again and again.

Anxiety

Anxiety is the most common emotion for people with time management issues. You may feel overwhelmed by your workload. You may worry about making mistakes. You may dread disappointing your coworkers or having a conflict with your manager. Time management failures like these create constant pressure.

Anxiety is a distraction. Instead of focusing on your work, you're focused on your fears. The only way to alleviate this kind of anxiety is to design a time management system that supports a high-quality work product.

But anxiety can also come from another source. Often, we feel anxiety when a task is difficult, and this kind of anxiety is usually accompanied by feelings of shame or inadequacy. We feel that we should know how to complete a task quickly and do it well just because it's been assigned to us. Your best next step is to proactively communicate your concerns. You may be surprised to find that your coworkers are happy to help.

Frustration

Frustration is one of the few emotions people feel comfortable expressing at work—primarily because of its inevitability. Frustration is a natural reaction to friction, and everyone experiences friction at work.

No one is immune to occasional disagreements, resource scarcity, disappointing outcomes, or challenging relationships. Improving your time management systems, communication skills, and interpersonal relationships can make a huge difference in how frequently you feel frustrated. What if the prevailing emotion at work is still frustration (or anger) even after improvements? In that case, the job itself may be a bad fit.

Happiness or Excitement

When work makes you happy or excited, it's a sign of alignment. It means you're doing work you enjoy with the resources and systems you need for success. Try to identify what is making you happy and why, and use that knowledge to improve other aspects of your work.

Maybe you like nitty-gritty details, such as marking up a document and fixing all the grammatical errors. Perhaps you find making spreadsheets for your projects enjoyable rather than tedious. Or perhaps forecasting market trends is so much fun that it doesn't seem like work. No matter your emotions at work, make sure you're examining them instead of suppressing them. Feelings are part of the human condition, and you're still human—even after you clock in.

Your Work Schedule

Have you ever wondered where the term "prime time" comes from? The answer reveals one of the best time management techniques around.

Television broadcasters match programs to time slots where they'll be most successful by breaking the days of the week and the times of the day into "dayparts" and identifying the qualities of those dayparts. This is why children's shows play on Saturday mornings and big-budget dramas on weekday evenings.

Use dayparting to supercharge your productivity. Categorize the different types of work you do and identify when you do that work best: your prime time. Try matching tasks with the times that best fit their needs. This dayparting strategy works best when you take into account both the differences in the time of day and the days of the week.

Mornings are prime time for Grace, a general manager at a hotel. It's when she has the most drive and focus. She also finds that energy and urgency come most naturally toward the beginning of her workweek. But her schedule doesn't align with when she does her best work, and her productivity is suffering.

After speaking with her team and her supervisors, she is able to rearrange her schedule. Now she schedules cluster planning or brainstorming for Mondays, deep work for Tuesdays through Thursdays, and quick tasks and update meetings for Fridays. She also avoids meetings before 11 a.m., reserving that time for tasks that require concentration and creativity. By using the dayparting strategy, Grace ensures that her most important work happens at her prime time.

What if you don't have that kind of control over your schedule? Then it's time to communicate. Identify the stakeholders in the work you're trying to move around and talk to them. Explain your goal of being in the best headspace to do your work well and ask if they can help. You may be surprised at people's flexibility.

Need help starting the conversation? The following is a template you can adapt. It lays out the challenge, presents an alternative, and opens the floor for collaborative problem-solving.

Hi Lloyd,

I was taking a look at my schedule and my to-do list and it got me thinking about the planning meeting we have on Monday mornings. That meeting requires creative thinking that I do best toward the end of the week. I was wondering if we could check in with the rest of the team and see if others feel similarly. If so, would you consider moving the meeting to Thursday or Friday?

Thanks for the consideration,

Sylvie

Finding Balance

Balance starts with boundaries. No matter how much you rework your schedule and reimagine your priorities, there will be times when you have to say, "I can't today." Setting and enforcing healthy boundaries is an essential time management skill. If you put your life in your company's hands, you will probably not like the schedule it gives you. Even progressive, employee-centric companies will take every minute you give them.

You can take breaks each day, work a reasonable number of hours each week, and take vacations while still fulfilling the job's expectations. But your company is not going to create this balance. You have to create it for yourself.

What about the 16 hours a day you spend away from work? Often, when people imagine work-life balance, they see a perfect day where every personal and professional priority fits neatly in 24 hours. This is an unrealistic and unhealthy expectation. It is simply impossible to find time for everything each day. However, balance becomes much easier to achieve if you lengthen your time horizon.

Instead of trying to cram everything into a day, consider how you can invest time into each of your priorities over a week or a month. If the quantity and duration of your daily tasks aren't realistic, get creative. Break down that priority into something smaller that works better as a daily commitment, or spread it out over multiple days or weeks.

These are the kinds of adjustments that could help Chelsea from our story in the beginning of the chapter. With proper time management and work-life balance, she can have enough mental space to plan, execute, and review her work—without letting down her boss Greg, her team, or her clients. You'll have to experiment with different arrangements and find what works best for you.

TWO

Manage Your Time by Managing Your Space

In this chapter, I explore ways to free up your brain to do work instead of managing it. Three themes come up repeatedly in this chapter: customization, iteration, and perseverance. Each person and work environment has a unique set of demands, preferences, challenges, and goals. A cookie-cutter approach won't work. Use this framework as a starting point, but adjust it to fit your needs.

We'll start by building the first iteration of a system that allows you to keep everything organized, prioritized, and accessible with minimal effort. The open office and the home office have different pitfalls and opportunities, so we'll outline the common challenges with these work contexts.

We'll also explore how to be productive in "third spaces," such as coffee shops and coworking spaces. Lastly, we'll discuss how to use meetings efficiently by avoiding common pitfalls that waste time, energy, and effort.

"Totally Disorganized on Tuesday"

Mitch is a teaching assistant at a local university. He supports Ariel, a professor of political science. They both split their time working from home and on campus. But that's where their similarities end.

Ariel is teaching four classes this semester, is working on her fifth book, and does media appearances on political radio and television shows. To Mitch, this seems like an impossible amount of work to do at all—let alone well. Yet Ariel is consistently sharp, organized, and punctual. It seems like she always has it together.

Mitch is a mess but can't seem to figure out why. He's juggling his graduate studies and his teaching assistant position—a fair amount of work, to be sure, but it shouldn't feel like a constant mental sprint. After three back-to-back all-nighters grading papers and working on his own research, the exhaustion catches up with him. He sleeps through his alarm and misses both of Ariel's morning classes.

He wakes up in a panic and reaches for his phone. Four missed calls and six text messages from Ariel. She is going to kill him.

"I'm so sorry," he frantically texts back, "I missed my alarm. I know it's not an excuse."

The response comes immediately: "Meet me at my office at 3."

A few hours later, Mitch arrives about 10 minutes early and spends each one rehearsing his apology. When Ariel walks in, it launches out of him. But before he can get out half a dozen words, she stops him.

"Just tell me what happened. Exactly."

She is her usual blunt self but doesn't seem angry. Mitch explains the all-nighters and the missed alarm as she nods and takes notes. Mitch finds it odd that she doesn't seem upset, but he focuses on his goal of making sure Ariel knows this won't happen again.

"Mitch, do you ever wonder how I do all this?" She gestures toward her wall of achievements. It's covered in diplomas, book covers, awards, and photos with influential political figures.

"All the time," he says. "It seems like an impossible amount of work."

"It's not impossible. It requires two things: organization and discipline. I know you have discipline. It's apparent in the quality of your work, and I can tell you're brilliant. But," Ariel leans forward, "you are not organized. And if you're going to be my TA, that needs to change. How do you keep track of what you need to do?"

Mitch pulls out a battered planner with a jumble of sticky notes poking out. "Stop." Ariel raises her hand and points at the shabby notebook. "That is not working. How do you keep track of your classes and appointments?"

He feels his cheeks heat as he glances at the planner again. Ariel raises her eyebrows, "That is not working, either. Where do you do your work?"

Mitch shrugs. "Sometimes at the faculty offices, sometimes at Martin Library, sometimes at home. Wherever I am."

"Okay." Ariel extends her open hand toward Mitch. "Let's start with that notebook."

Using Technology to Your Advantage

As I mentioned in chapter one, our brains were optimized to find food, shelter, and community to stay alive. Achieving these goals in prehistoric societies required focus, creativity, problem-solving, communication, and imagination—skills we use at work every day. But our hunter-gatherer ancestors did not need productivity.

Productivity is a new demand placed on us. But it's hard to be productive if all you have is a caveman's brain. Remembering all the dates and details associated with modern work doesn't play to your brain's strengths.

Technology can bridge the gap between what your brain is designed to do and what needs to be done. It can help you remember details, remind you of deadlines, help you focus, and keep you accountable. But don't expect any random tool to solve your time management problems. Choose your technology wisely and implement it well.

Time Masters take this decision seriously because productivity tools have downsides, too. The wrong one can be distracting or overwhelming, or feel like another thing you don't have time to do. Time Masters make sure to choose tools that fit their goals, preferences, and context. With so many options, you don't have to settle for something that doesn't fit your needs.

Embracing the Central Management System

You'll probably need more than one tool to manage all of work's moving pieces. I have yet to find one tool that does it all well. Tools that claim to do everything tend to be mediocre generalists and cost more time than they save. Instead, focus on finding specialist tools that are excellent at solving the particular productivity problems you face.

Once you've identified the right tools, integrate them into a central management system. A central management system allows you to easily store, organize, and retrieve what you need to do your job efficiently and effectively. Your tools don't need to digitally talk to each other (though it helps when they do). They need to connect in your mind and habits.

It may take some effort to get your tools configured and learn how to get the most out of them. But the right tools make staying organized feel natural and seamless. They free up the brain's resources for doing work instead of managing it.

Organizing Your Tasks

Every job is a set of relevant tasks that need to be done consistently. But for most people, the details change daily. Sometimes by a little. Sometimes by a lot. Keeping track of those details is an essential part of time management.

For every task you're assigned, you need to know:

- What are the task's requirements?

- What tools or materials do you need to complete it?

- How long will the task take to complete?

- When is it due?

- How important is the task?

Sometimes, the answers to these questions will come intuitively. But if there's even a glimmer of uncertainty, double-check with your colleagues or supervisor. You might feel bashful about not knowing the answer and hesitate to ask, but your colleagues will appreciate your diligence.

Organizing Your Time

Once your tasks are organized, you need to fit them all into your dayparts. Haphazardly cramming tasks into your schedule is a recipe for a stressful week where you don't get much done. Commit to two simple practices to ensure you're working on the right things at the right times.

The first is the 4Ns approach to prioritization. Take a look at the tasks on your list. Decide whether each task is urgent, important, both, or neither.

1. Now. The tasks that are rated both important and urgent should be done as soon as possible. Make as much progress as you can before moving on.

2. Next. Tasks that are important but not urgent should be done next. It's useful to schedule these to a specific date and time. At that time, these tasks become urgent.

3. Not by me (or not by myself). Tasks that are urgent but not important should be delegated or distributed. If you are a leader, you may want to delegate these tasks to a team member. If you're an individual contributor, you may want to ask for help with these tasks.

4. Never. Tasks that are neither urgent nor important should be ignored. Make sure you have clarity on both urgency and importance. If you're not sure, get confirmation.

The second practice is deep work blocks. Some tasks are best completed during an extended period of uninterrupted work. During these times, ruthlessly remove distractions. Turn off all your notifications, close any unnecessary programs, and politely dissuade colleagues from interrupting you. Laser focus your attention on a singular task until it's complete or your deep work period has ended.

If calendar blocking is new to you, let your supervisor know it's something you'd like to try. Start with shorter periods at a low frequency, such as 30 minutes twice a week. Put those blocks of deep work on your calendar and respect them like they were meetings with your CEO. Give your team and your supervisor a heads up before you disappear and make sure you can report progress.

As deep work blocks show their value, you'll want to do more of them. But remember, deep work is mentally taxing. There's a limit to how much you can do in one sitting or in one day. Listen to your body. If you start to feel mentally drained, you're piling on too much.

Streamline through Digital Tools

Now you have some strategies for managing your tasks and your time. But what tools should you use to get that done?

You've probably used analog tools such as notepads, planners, or sticky notes in the past. They have one advantage over digital tools: You remember what you write better than what you type. For some situations, taking physical notes may be preferable, but remember Mitch's mess of sticky notes in our opening story? That's no way to balance a complex set of tasks. In most contexts, the benefit of better recall with a paper planner is outweighed by its disadvantages.

Analog tools are only useful when they're with you, and they're easy to lose or leave behind. They aren't searchable. If your handwriting isn't the best, you may have trouble reading your notes. If you need to make a change, you'll waste time rewriting. And lastly, it's challenging to collaborate with others using analog tools.

Digital tools have none of these disadvantages. My personal and professional experience with honing time management skills leads me to recommend using digital tools to build your management system. Start with what your company provides. Most companies use Microsoft Office or Google Suite for email and workplace software. Become an expert in these tools and use them to make the first iteration of your management system.

Calendar

Your calendar exists to give structure to your day, so use it that way. The following are five of my favorite tactics for organizing and protecting your time.

1. **Defend your most important hours.** When your colleagues look at your calendar, they see what's free and what's busy. They can't see your meeting preferences. Set up a recurring block for the first and last hours of the day for planning purposes and an hour in the middle for a lunch break.

2. **Note your dayparts.** As you start to understand which dayparts are best suited to different types of work, it's useful to plug those dayparts into your calendar. Make sure to set these calendar events as "free," so you don't accidentally block

off your entire week. If this makes your calendar look too messy, consider creating an additional calendar view so you can toggle it off when you don't need it.

3. Schedule regular deep work time. As mentioned, deep work blocks are a powerful productivity tool. Once you and your supervisor are comfortable with them, try scheduling them at regular intervals.

4. Invest in a scheduling tool. If you schedule meetings often, you probably lose time going back and forth over email. Collaborative scheduling tools like Doodle allow you to propose several options for attendees to vote on. Direct schedulers like Calendly or Acuity Scheduling create a link that external attendees can use to put a meeting straight onto their calendar.

5. Poke around in your settings. Customization of Google Calendar and Microsoft Outlook can support your productivity in powerful ways. For example, you can change the default event reminder in both tools. This can be a game-changer if one of your time management challenges is being late to meetings. For more examples of technical tweaks to try, visit betterwithphoebe.com/calendarhacks.

Task Manager

Avoid using a Word or Google document or your email inbox as your to-do list. I've seen too many clients get bogged down this way. Email isn't designed with task ranking in mind. A good task manager allows you to easily organize, prioritize, and contextualize tasks. You may be able to set up a document or inbox to do this, but it will likely be more challenging and more prone to failure than if you use a purpose-built tool.

Google and Microsoft both include task managers with their work software suites. If you've never used a task manager before, start with Google Tasks or Microsoft To Do to learn about your needs and preferences. These tools are lean on features so they're easy to learn, but that also means they may not be the best long-term solutions.

You'll likely identify the gaps over time and want to upgrade to a more powerful tool. Options such as Trello, Asana, and Todoist have features that allow you to organize tasks more dynamically and store them with more context. You may want to invest in the premium versions of these tools to access more features. I have used Todoist to organize my tasks for years. The time it saves me is worth 1,000 times more than what I pay for my premium subscription. For more information on how I use Todoist to stay productive, visit betterwithphoebe.com/todoist.

Maximizing Productivity in an Open Office

I'll say what we're all thinking: Open offices are not good for getting work done. They were ostensibly designed to promote communication and collaboration. Designers thought the lack of walls would create an environment ripe for spontaneous interactions between coworkers. But they do the exact opposite.

Of course, by the end of 2020, the very concept of an office at all—much less an open office—was turned on its head with the COVID-19 pandemic. With an estimated 42 percent of the American workforce working from home during the crisis, America suddenly became a work-from-home economy.

Because of the pandemic experience, it's possible that the very concept of offices—open or not—will look different as corporate America rethinks its approach to work. What makes an office work from a time management perspective applies whether you work from there or from home. There are numerous distractions in both spaces that you'll have to identify and minimize.

As for open offices, they're spaces where we're less likely to interact with our coworkers face-to-face and more likely to get sick. Just about every scientific study that examines the impact of open offices on productivity finds that it makes people feel distracted, exhausted, and surveilled. So why do companies keep designing these modern-day torture devices? They're cheap.

While the pandemic has upended the future of the modern workspace and changed the prevailing view of the open office, it's likely that offices will continue to be a fixture of the American corporate environment in one way or another well into the future. And while you can't change your office's layout, you can change its impact on your productivity with some specific steps.

Go in with a Plan

When you arrive at the office, your mission should be to get started on your first task as quickly as possible. But mornings in an office are full of time traps. Let's explore how to avoid some of them so you can get started promptly.

Refrain from endless chitchat.

Watercooler chat is a useful way to build workplace relationships. But it's easy to get caught up talking and lose precious morning momentum. Be polite, but don't let conversations go on too long.

If you feel stuck in a conversation, it's okay to jump in and say, "Sorry to interrupt you, but I need to get started on this big report. Can I catch up with you later?" Your colleague will understand. You are both there to get a job done.

Avoid the email black hole.

Many people make the mistake of starting their day stuck in their inbox. When you do this, you spend your best hours working through a list of everyone else's priorities. Limit how much time you spend on email.

In the morning, limit your email time to a "fire scan." This is a quick check to identify any important and urgent emails and to see if they represent a top-priority task. If there are no "fires," close your email and start working on the top-priority tasks in your task manager tool.

Later, you should do a thorough cleanup of your inbox to identify which emails represent tasks to be completed and which are noise. Remember, your inbox is not a task manager. If an email is a task, add it to your task manager with context.

The inbox is a dangerous place for people trying to manage their time well. Try to limit how often you clean your inbox. If you go into your inbox to retrieve work materials, don't get distracted by your unread count. Get out of the danger zone quickly.

It can be helpful to choose specific times to check email. I like to do a fire scan in the morning, a cleanup before lunch, and a combination scan/cleanup before leaving for the day. Everyone is different. Experiment and figure out what minimum is appropriate for your job.

You've escaped the morning obstacle course and have made it to your desk. Now what? Use your management system to turn your workday into a plan. Resist the temptation to plan at the beginning of your day, because that's when you have the most natural motivation to get things done. Instead, set aside 15 to 30 minutes toward the end of your workday for planning the next one. Here are four things to do at the end of your day:

Start by looking back.
Are there any tasks you meant to accomplish that day that didn't fit? If so, reprioritize and schedule them. Communicate with stakeholders if necessary. Are there any new requests to organize? If so, make sure you have all the context you need and schedule them into a future day.

Review your calendar.
Do you have any meetings? Do you need to do or assemble anything to prepare for them? If so, add that as a task in your manager. How much free work time do you have? What kind of work is suited to that time?

Look at your task manager.
Double-check the priority of each pending task. Upgrade or downgrade as necessary. Look at the tasks scheduled for the next day and estimate how long each will take. Ensure that the total amount of required time is one to two hours less than the total amount of free work time you have. If the required time is too high, reschedule tasks and communicate with stakeholders about any delays.

Prepare your workstation.
Identify the first thing you want to work on in the morning. Make sure all the necessary tools or materials will be ready when you sit down so you can get started immediately. Identify the materials you'll need for the day's other tasks. Make sure they're easily accessible but not distracting. Give your workstation a quick tidying up. It should feel welcoming when you sit down in the morning.

Think about how some of these changes could apply to Mitch from the beginning of this chapter. Even though he doesn't always work from a physical office, he would greatly benefit from setting up the next day's work ahead of time. If he were to look back at what he did and didn't do, organize his calendar for the next day, and check in with Ariel about new tasks, he'd be prepared for a successful day of work—before it began.

It's a big list of changes to make at once. The most sustainable way to get to this ideal workflow is to choose one to three tactics to focus on first. Once they become habits, come back to this list and add a new tactic.

Use Interactions to Your Advantage

Your workplace relationships are your most important time management tools. It's great when we simply "click" with colleagues, and strong workplace relationships do sometimes happen by accident. More often, however, they have to be built with intention.

A relationship works well when it's effective in three areas: expectations, boundaries, and collaboration. Let's discuss how to leverage each of these so your workplace interactions support your time management goals, and find out how they relate to a big time suck: meetings.

Expectations

Work is rarely a solo endeavor. We depend on others, and others depend on us to accomplish the overall goals of the company. But how do we do that seamlessly when we each have different needs and preferences? It starts with communicating expectations clearly and up-front.

When you receive a task from others or give one to someone else, everyone should have the same understanding of the expectations. Clarifying the following details will save time and frustration for everyone involved:

- When is it due?

- What elements are required for it to be considered complete?

- What does quality look like?

- How much time should a task take?

- How difficult should it be?

- How important is the task?

- Why is the task important for the organization?

This expectation-setting step creates an opportunity to proactively communicate needs or preferences and identify potential problems.

Collaboration

Maybe a task is a high priority for your colleague but not for you. Or the finished product they have in mind is too time-consuming to fit on your plate. What do you do if your needs or preferences conflict with others'? Work together to find a solution that meets as many needs as possible. This is collaborative problem-solving.

When you need to negotiate the details of a task, your first step should be to make sure everyone clearly understands the reasons for the various preferences at play. Focusing on what you're trying to achieve instead of how you're trying to get there allows for alternative paths to be explored. This is how you can efficiently collaborate to reach an outcome with which everyone is happy.

Boundaries

Collaborative problem-solving is not a cure-all. There will be times when you aren't able to close the gap between preferences. When this happens, it's crucial that everyone involved can tactfully communicate boundaries. Suppose a task creates an unreasonable burden or puts you in a bind. In that case, you have a responsibility to yourself and your work product to respectfully say no.

Learn what your boundaries should be and how to communicate them in a way that will be respected and received well within your company's culture. For some people, setting boundaries is a scary prospect. But with a little courage, practice, and some feedback from trusted colleagues, anyone can do it. Setting boundaries at work is a skill that can be learned and, eventually, mastered.

Meetings

These are meant to be a time investment that pays off. Yet they have a terrible reputation for being a waste of time. It's not because meetings themselves are bad. It's because most people don't run them well.

The perfect meeting checks off the following criteria:

○ Has a clear agenda or purpose

○ Is scheduled for the minimum length of time

○ Invites relevant people

- Does not invite irrelevant people

- Provides invitees any materials they need to be prepared, with enough time to review them

- Starts on time

- Stays on schedule

- Recaps decisions and action items before it ends

- Ends on time

- Provides a summary to all relevant parties

While we're unlikely to have the pleasure of attending perfect meetings, you can strive to make sure your own meetings have as many of these qualities as possible. When you set a meeting, you can control most of these variables. But what about meetings run by others?

This comes back to expectations, collaboration, and boundaries. If a meeting seems to be in danger of wasting time, identify which features are missing. Communicate your expectations to the organizer, ask to collaborate on how to solve the problem, and set a boundary if the organizer is unwilling or unable to resolve the issue.

Time Management for the Remote Office

Prior to 2020, many workers hadn't experienced working remotely. Then came a pandemic, and just about everyone with an office job suddenly found themselves working out of their home. Knowing how to work effectively and productively from home is an important skill. US employers have been gradually becoming more comfortable with allowing their employees to telecommute. As the corona-virus pandemic forced many employers into a remote work experiment, two critical lessons emerged.

First, many skeptics found that their companies were able to operate without an office. Second, those naysay-ers realized that the open office concept has nothing on a remote workforce when it comes to cost savings. While some employers rushed to get their workers back into an office despite the health risk, others adopted more flexible approaches. Some added remote work as a permanent option for employees. Others got rid of their offices alto-gether. Even if you're not working remotely now, you may find yourself working from home sometime soon.

Whether it's from home, a hotel, a coffee shop, or a coworking space, working remotely has specific chal-lenges. Many find that working from home comes with a steep learning curve with regards to productivity. The tools you learned about working in an open office are useful for a home environment, too, but avoiding common pitfalls requires a few more adjustments.

Working from Home

My coaching clients who are new to working from home tend to have the same problems. They fail to keep healthy, productive working hours, working either too much or not enough. They struggle to keep up their energy and motiva-tion. Their mental and physical health slips. They grapple with unreasonable expectations from family. They get stir-crazy. They're endlessly distracted. All of it wastes time.

It's not that remote work is bad; it just requires a dif-ferent approach. As a remote worker, it's possible to stay healthy, keep your energy up, manage your time effectively, and become even more productive than your office-bound colleagues. Avoid the pitfalls that Mitch, from the beginning of this chapter, experienced. Instead of working odd hours to your detriment and losing track of tasks, you can establish a work-friendly schedule and a workspace that sets you up for success.

Create an efficient environment.

Many work-from-home newbies fail to set up an ergonomic workstation. You have control over this space, so don't be cheap or lazy and spend 40 hours a week slouching on your couch. Trust me, the inevitable back and neck pain isn't worth it. Use the principles from the physical work environment section in chapter one to create an ergonomic workstation.

The ideal scenario is to have a dedicated home office that you can outfit. But many people don't have a spare room. If a separate home office isn't possible, get creative. Small investments can make a massive difference in your physical comfort and your productivity. For a guide to creating an ergonomic workstation at home, visit betterwithphoebe.com/perfecthomeoffice.

Don't forget to ask your supervisor if the company offers reimbursement for any home office setup expenses; many do.

Set your working hours.

Most remote workers keep standard business hours. It's smart to reclaim some of the time you'd spend getting ready or commuting for other priorities, like sleep. But it's a bad idea to roll out of bed minutes before the workday begins. Working from home is not an excuse to be unprofessional. Always start the day fueled and fully alert.

If you have a flexible schedule, you can set your hours around your natural energy cycle. However, the lack of structure and accountability creates challenges. You might find it hard to get everything done because you're working too little. Or you might feel exhausted because you're working too much.

Get in the habit of logging your work hours. Each week, compare your hours worked to tasks completed and what's considered standard for the job. Experiment with different schedules until you find the one that fits.

Take breaks to recharge.

Your colleagues know you're working when they can see you at your desk. But how do they know you're working when you're behind a screen and miles away? If you're new to working from home, you might feel awkward, guilty, or nervous about taking breaks.

This is a common reaction. You may be scared that people will think your absences are conspicuous or excessive or that they might forget you're there. Don't work endless hours without breaks. Instead, identify the critical stakeholders in your work. Speak with them daily—even if it's just small talk. Schedule a meeting with them at least once per month to give updates, brainstorm ideas, or solve problems.

Whether you're working a standard or flexible schedule, it's vital that you take breaks, lunches, and vacations. Breaks are essential time management tools, not indulgences. Your brain needs them. Your body needs them. Your work needs them. They're the difference between burning out and getting things done.

Experiment and figure out what kinds of breaks meet your needs while still falling within what's appropriate in your company's culture. Remember, your productivity habits need to work in the long run. Working prolonged hours without breaks isn't sustainable.

Tip: Is It Time to Rent an Office or Shared Space?

Should your "third space" be an office rental? If more than two of the following are true, you may want to explore a coworking space or office rental:

- The advice in the previous section isn't improving your productivity.
- Your job requires regular, in-person meetings with clients or collaborators.
- Regular networking opportunities would improve your work.
- You need physical space for equipment or materials.
- You deeply miss having "work friends."

Costs can vary depending on your location, the type of rental, and the perks of your membership. Here are five factors to keep in mind:

- Needs: What are your goals? Does the space achieve them?
- Location: Is the commute doable? Are your preferred amenities close by?
- Equipment: What is provided? What will you have to bring?
- Perks: Does it provide membership benefits? Will you use them?
- Comparative cost: Are you getting a good value?

Maintaining Productivity at Home

I've been working from home for more than six years. During that time, I've learned a few more unconventional practices that make working from home more successful. In the beginning, I consistently found myself isolated, frustrated, unproductive, and physically uncomfortable. This is the case for many work-from-home newbies. They often blame it on the format and say these issues are inherent to working remotely. But that's not true.

Working from home is a set of workplace skills just like pivot tables or public speaking. To do it successfully, you must learn the skills, practice them, and master them. It took me a while to understand where I was going wrong and what practices could help me stay productive. It took a while longer to turn those practices into habits. But once I did, working from home became a joy.

The same is true for my clients who struggle in their first remote job. Once they understand the problems, find the right solutions, and turn those solutions into habits, they're able to fully enjoy working from home.

Set explicit expectations with the people you live with.

I am well aware that parents of young children struggled to work from home during the pandemic. Young kids, attending school at home over Zoom and needing IT help or simply asking questions during their parents' virtual meetings, isn't the type of interruptions I'm talking about here.

The people you live with—roommates, family members, or romantic partners—see you in a home context, and may expect you to behave the way you do during your downtime. They might ask you to do chores, errands, or other tasks when your attention needs to be on work. They might interrupt you when you're in the thick of a task.

The mismatch in expectations can create tension and conflict in otherwise balanced relationships—especially if your housemates don't have experience working from home. Thankfully, these issues are preventable with a simple conversation.

Make sure everyone knows what to expect from you during work hours. Explain what your hours are and what you need during them, and get specific about what you can and can't do when you're on the clock. Ask them about their needs, and collaborate to design a scheme where everyone feels their time and priorities are respected.

Minimize home-specific distractions.
One of the most significant disadvantages of working from home is your proximity to extremely potent distractions. All of your favorite activities are a few paces away, and there's no peer pressure from colleagues to help you stay on task.

Notice how often the most common home-specific distractions steal your attention:

- Interactions with members of your household

- Trips to the kitchen

- Chores and errands

- Recreational phone apps, such as games and social media

- Recreational media, such as television or podcasts

We'll explore distraction more fully in chapter three, including how to deal with home-specific distractions.

Keep your personal life organized.
Chores, errands, and other personal to-dos can be powerful distractions. Reduce their ability to distract by applying
your work-related time management skills to your personal
life. Get into the habit of adding personal tasks to a manager and scheduling them. It's okay to use the same
manager for work and personal tasks if you can separate
them within the app.

Certain personal tasks are more distracting than others.
Try to get those done before your workday. If a new task
comes up, avoid doing it right away. During your working
hours, all personal tasks are distractions—even otherwise productive activities like cleaning. Note any new
tasks in your personal task manager and set a time to
get them done.

Create "commute" rituals.
As you physically commute to the office, your mind shifts.
You step out of your relaxed, personal mindset into your
focused, professional mindset. How can you re-create this
benefit without spending half an hour in traffic? By creating
routines that support that mental transition.

Commute rituals can elaborate or simple. One of my
clients' commute rituals was lighting a candle before opening her laptop and blowing it out after closing the laptop.
Another client, who had a home office, liked to take three
deep breaths before going in and three more after closing
the door at the end of the day. The important part of your
commute ritual is to do it every day.

Pay attention to your health.
The healthier you are, the easier it is to be productive.
Unfortunately, working from home sets you up for a
more sedentary lifestyle than working from an office.

Small activities like grabbing something from the printer or heading out for a coffee add movement to an otherwise stationary day.

While the benefits of hitting the gym can't be denied, a workout isn't the only way to incorporate activity into your day. Simple practices like standing up regularly, stretching, and taking walks can impact your physical and mental health.

Don't forget about food. Where there are offices, there are restaurants and cafes. But when you're working from home, you may have fewer options. Don't rely on takeout, delivery, frozen food, or boxed snacks. Instead, grow your cooking skills so your body and mind are well-fueled.

Seek out alternative workspaces.
Just because you're able to work from home doesn't mean you have to work from your house every day. It's useful to have a workspace outside of the home that works with your needs and preferences. Likely, your mind went to a coffee shop. But there are lots of suitable "third spaces." Check out libraries, hotel lobbies, museums, and university campuses. You might find that your favorite park, mall, gym, or restaurant has connectivity options.

THREE

Time-Proven Strategies = Time-Management Results

You've set the table for excellent time management. You've dabbled in best practices. Now, it's time to go deep into the strategies that will make you a Time Master. In this chapter, I dive into proven techniques for setting goals, breaking bad habits, and keeping bulletproof prioritization.

As you incorporate these techniques into your daily responsibilities, you'll notice that you have a significant increase in clarity, passion, and efficiency around your work. Some tools may seem tedious or difficult initially, but the friction is just a natural function of learning something new.

You're learning a new skill, so be patient and commit to giving each method a real shot. Stick with each for at least two weeks, evaluating when they become more manageable and when you start to notice results.

"In the Weeds on Wednesday"

Myles can't stop saying yes.

He's not a pushover. He just gets joy out of helping people. He's a team player, and his can-do attitude makes him one of the most well-liked programmers on the team. He replies to every request with a ready smile and friendly agreement, but cracks are forming.

Myles never knows how he'll get it all done. He spends each day juggling tasks for others with the core responsibilities of his job.

And here comes Paula again. He puts on a smile as she approaches, bracing for the next request. She wants help with quality assurance on some code for her client's project. Myles isn't on the QA team anymore. But he doesn't want the company to push lousy code, so he says yes, and his to-do list gets a little longer. Maybe he can work on it during the planning meeting later that afternoon.

Cece, his product manager, starts the meeting the same way she always does. She walks the team through the updates to the product road map, noting the most significant changes.

"Myles?"

His head shoots up as he realizes Cece is calling on him.

"So glad you're with us, Myles." She cracks a sarcastic smile. "When should we expect the mock-ups for the new interface?" He hesitates as he realizes he doesn't know the answer. He hasn't prepared for the meeting.

Cece senses Myles is at a loss and throws him a lifeline, "Let's circle back to that a bit later, okay?" He breathes a silent sigh of relief and digs into his email for the information. Thirty-eight unread messages. How did it build up so quickly? He responds to a few, then realizes that Cece is calling on him again. He can see Cece's annoyance, but she bails him out again. "Just drop those dates in the team chat when you have them," she says.

The rest of the meeting is uneventful, but Cece holds him back as everyone leaves the conference room. "Myles, why were you on Mars during that meeting? It's not like you."

He apologizes for not preparing, explaining that he'd been proofreading a memo as a favor for his buddy Venkatesh and had lost track of time working on it. He then explains that his lack of attentiveness was due to working on Paula's QA project. He confesses to getting caught up in his email when he should have been pulling the information she asked for.

With each explanation, Cece gets more annoyed. "Myles, you are a UX designer. Your job is not to do Venkatesh's memo or Paula's QA. Your job isn't email. Your job is to design great interfaces. Sometimes you just have to say no."

Cece is right. Myles knows he says yes too often. No wonder he is so stressed and behind. He is simply taking on too much.

"I like helping people, Cece! I hate letting people down," Myles says, looking down at his feet. "I want people to feel like they can depend on me."

Cece puts her hand on his shoulder, "I'm your boss, Myles. I'm the one who needs to feel like I can depend on you. Focus on your job. Prioritize your work first. It's okay for other people's stuff to wait. If anyone has a problem with that, they can talk to me."

Work SMARTer

The way you spend your time is a reflection of your priorities. But where do those priorities come from? When you succumb to distraction, you allow your subconscious to set your priorities. Your subconscious is always shifting. So when you let it run the show, you'll always be shifting, too.

This is why setting goals is so vital for time management. It's much easier to stay focused on a goal you consciously set. While many people set conscious daily goals, few set ones that are also effective. They're usually vague, reactive, negative, or unrealistic—a toxic cocktail.

Effective goals tend to have five characteristics in common. When goals are Specific, Measurable, Achievable, Relevant, and Timely, they are more likely to be achieved. These are commonly referred to as SMART goals. When planned accordingly, SMART goals weaken the psychological traps that prevent us from making lasting changes, building new habits, and persevering through adversity.

The SMART goals model was conceptualized in 1981 by George T. Doran, a management consultant. His version was designed to be a framework to help corporate leaders set goals for their businesses. So it's not surprising that this model works well (with a couple of tweaks) for individuals.

Specific

Specific goals are easier to achieve because they give clear direction. They point you toward a related set of distinct actions that build on each other. When a goal is specific, you can easily see what steps get you closer to achieving it.

Goals with a high success probability occupy a specific-ity sweet spot—specific enough to give direction but broad enough to provide flexibility. Most clients come to me with a goal that is vague, reactive, negative, or unrealistic. My first job as their coach is to get them into the sweet spot.

We start with an exercise to give their goals more substance. It also neutralizes some of the psychological poison found in toxic goals by reorienting their mindset toward the future.

1. Identify at least one thing that, if true, means you are succeeding at the goal.

2. Identify at least one thing that, if true, means you are failing at the goal.

3. Associate each of your success signs with at least one action that supports it.

4. Associate each of your failure signs with at least one action that reduces it.

We then use the answers to rewrite the client's goal into a specific, action-oriented one. Think of these prompts as a specificity formula. Let's start with an example you can use right now.

Since you're reading this book, you likely want to improve your time management. "I want to improve my time management" is a vague goal. If you answered the four prompts in the exercise, you might come up with some-thing like this:

○ Completing tasks on time is a sign of success.

○ Being late to meetings is a sign of failure.

- Recording tasks with full context supports completing tasks on time.

- Keeping my calendar visible reduces how often I'm late to meetings.

When you revise your goal, it might look like this: "I want to improve my time management by completing tasks on time and not being late for meetings. To do this, I will record tasks with full context and keep my calendar visible."

This version describes distinct actions that create desired outcomes and avoid undesired outcomes. Now your goal clearly outlines what success looks like and how to get there.

Measurable

Once you've made your goal specific, how will you know how you're doing? Consider how you'll track your progress. Is there something you can count, grade, or rate as pass/fail?

It might make sense to keep an exact count for some criteria. On-time attendance at meetings is easy to rate and track. Either you were on time or you were not. You can count how many times you were late and record it.

Adding tasks with context is more challenging to measure efficiently. In this case, it might make sense do a check-in at the end of the day and ask yourself how often you had to track down context at the last minute. Consistently record your responses to see your improvement over time.

Remember Howard, our project manager from chapter one? His time management issues had him so stressed that they were causing marital problems. As he works on his time management, he might also incorporate stress management into his goal. How would he measure how much stress he was bringing home?

He could count specific activities that indicate calmness, like conflict-free evenings. He could track stress management behaviors like meditation. He could ask his wife to give him a weekly rating on how much she felt his work stress impacted their relationship. While Howard's emotional state isn't exactly quantifiable, he can still get creative to make his goal measurable.

Once your goal is specific and measurable, it's a good idea to see if it's binary and how that should inform your approach to achieving it. A binary goal is one that has no gray area. Quitting smoking is a binary goal. Either you have quit or you are still smoking.

Binary goals can set you up to abandon a goal prematurely. Progressive goals give you more space to fail, learn, and grow. If you have a setback on a progressive goal, it's easy to just see it as a speed bump. But with binary goals, setbacks can feel very emotionally impactful. "I failed" can easily become "I'm a failure."

If your goals are binary, try to reframe them so they focus on progress instead of perfection. If the goal must be binary, remember that setbacks are normal and commit to persevering when things get challenging.

Achievable

Your goals should be realistic. They should be within reach for someone with your resources and skill level. And, most importantly, the elements of success should be within your control or influence.

People are often discouraged from setting conservative goals that can be easily achieved. Instead, they are encouraged to develop challenging "stretch goals." Proponents of stretch goals believe they make us more ambitious, inspired, and hardworking. "Stretching" is excellent for goals where you have plenty of resources, experience, or innate interest. But I don't recommend them for beginners. When you're new to something or struggling with it, setting stretch goals usually backfires.

Chelsea, our software developer from chapter one, had trouble with many aspects of time management. She struggled to accurately estimate her workload, which led to missed deadlines and rushed deliverables with errors. Given her current situation, a goal of "beat all my deadlines with no errors" would certainly be an unrealistic stretch goal.

Because stretch goals require that we push ourselves to the limit, we risk burning out. Missing a stretch goal despite all that hard work can be painfully discouraging. On the other hand, starting with goals that are easy allows you to develop a track record of success. As you achieve your "easy goals," you build confidence and momentum. You can then start making your goals more challenging and begin reaching for stretch goals.

Instead of setting that unrealistic stretch goal, Chelsea should set a realistic goal, such as "reprioritize my tasks every day." That goal is within her ability and helps her improve her skills at estimating her workload accurately. She could then work toward a more challenging goal like "have my deliverables ready for review a day early."

Relevant

Is your goal connected to your company's objectives, your job's objectives, your life's objectives, or your personal values? When a goal has many points of connection, motivation comes more naturally. Instead of being something you have to do, it becomes something you want to do.

A goal connected to your personal values and life objectives generates the most powerful motivation. Any time you need to make a goal more relevant, use the Deep Whys exercise from chapter one:

1. What is happening?

2. How is this impacting me?

3. Why do I want to improve this?

Take a moment to review your notes from your first time doing the exercise. What did it bring up for you? Reviewing them makes you feel more motivated to improve your time management because you've connected it to your personal values and life objectives.

Timely

Goals should not be open-ended. They should have a particular start date and a particular end date, and the definition of success should match the amount of time provided to achieve it. This creates the urgency necessary to get started and keep up the momentum until the goal is achieved. This also allows you to create a plan with incremental milestones to help you see progress and stay motivated.

A binary goal such as "complete a project" might be broken into week-long chunks with specific, outcome-oriented milestones such as "submit a proposal" or "complete a mock-up." But a progressive goal like "improve my time management" doesn't lend itself to this kind of planning.

Instead of assigning specific, discrete achievements to dates, focus on process-oriented milestones. Go back to your list of actions from the Measurable step and set milestones based on completing them consistently.

If your goal was improving your time management in 90 days, you might break that into six separate 15-day challenges. During each challenge, you would focus on consistently performing well on a particular aspect of time management.

SMART Goals

S	**Specific** State exactly what you want to accomplish.
M	**Measurable** Create mini goals to measure your progress.
A	**Achievable** Is your goal within your scope and possible to accomplish?
R	**Relevant** Is the goal worthwhile to your job function?
T	**Timely** When you will get it done—be specific on data or time frame.

Remember to Revise and Reevaluate

After you've made your goal Specific, Measurable, Achievable, Relevant, and Timely, it's time to get started. As you're working on your goal, you may find that your context changes and your SMART goal is no longer feasible.

That's when you take your SMART goal and turn it into a SMARTER goal. The added "E" reminds you to consistently "Evaluate" your goal against your context. The "R" encourages you to proactively "Revise" it when necessary.

If you're experiencing friction while you work toward your goal, take a step back. Which aspect of your SMART criteria doesn't seem to be working? Does your approach need to change, or does your goal need to be adjusted? Once you understand the source of the friction, revise your goal so it's feasible again.

Adding Evaluate and Revise to the SMART framework helps you set effective goals that are also flexible enough to withstand the variables life throws at you.

Stop Multitasking

Many people think multitasking is productive. Employers will even list it as a desired skill in job descriptions. But multitasking is not a virtue. It's distraction masquerading as efficiency.

Imagine you're in charge of lighting a scene in a play. You have one powerful stage lamp at your disposal. You can widen the beam to take in the entire stage, or you can narrow it into a spotlight and focus on a single actor. But you can't do both. There's only one lamp, and it can only produce so much light.

The world around you is the stage, and your attention is the stage lamp.

Why Multitasking Doesn't Work

When your attention is focused, you notice every tiny detail about the object of your focus but miss most of what's happening around you. When your attention is wide, you notice most of what's happening around you but miss the detail. Multitasking is asking your brain to fully focus on multiple things at the same time. It's simply not capable of doing this.

You may think you're doing these tasks in parallel, but instead you're rapidly switching between them. Your brain can do rapid task-switching, but it's not the way it works best. Every time you switch tasks, you lose momentum. The more complex the tasks are, the more momentum you lose as you switch between them—and the worse you perform at the task.

Some tasks are so mindless that the loss in momentum doesn't matter, or performance isn't impacted in a meaningful way. Take, for example, walking down a familiar street while talking to a friend about a casual subject. Your brain is switching between listening, deciding what to say, saying it, and not stepping in the puddle.

Since these are all simple tasks, it's easy for your brain to switch tasks. But what if you didn't know where you were going, were discussing a complex subject, or were speaking with someone you wanted to impress? The rapid task-switching would become much more difficult.

This is why multitasking at work is such a bad idea. Work tasks are mentally demanding. You can't afford to lose momentum or perform poorly. But if you focus on one task at a time, you can get more done in less time with less energy and at a better quality.

Be aware of subconscious multitasking. When you need to focus on a complex task, all other demands force your brain to do rapid task-switching. If you're listening to music or a podcast, you have a TV on in the background, or you're talking with a coworker while you work, you're still reducing your brain's ability to build momentum and perform at a high level.

Break the Habit

Time Masters are keenly aware of the complexity and importance of the tasks they're assigned. They know multitasking reduces the speed and quality of their work, so they avoid it. But for many of us, multitasking is a habit. We slip into it without even realizing it. Let's explore how you can stop multitasking and start single-tasking.

In chapter two, we explored the concept of putting deep work blocks on your calendar. A deep work block is for working on one task, so it's the perfect time to practice single-tasking. Choose the task you want to focus on, get out all your necessary tools and materials, and ruthlessly eliminate all distractions—including anything you'd be tempted to multitask with.

At first, single-tasking during your deep work block might be difficult. But with each block, you'll get better at resisting the urge to multitask. You'll notice that you're making progress more quickly, you're happier with the result, and you want to spend more time in the deep work zone. You can't spend your entire day in a deep work cavern, isolated and unreachable. But you can apply some deep work practices to your regular working time to make single-tasking easier.

Adjust Your Expectations

A coworker drops by your desk, asking if you saw an email he sent 20 minutes prior. If you didn't see it because you were getting lunch, in a meeting, or on a conference call, you probably wouldn't feel bashful about saying so. But for some reason, we often feel uncomfortable explaining away a delay with our jobs' actual duties.

Give yourself permission to treat your daily work with the same level of importance. If you find yourself pestered by an impatient colleague, simply say, "I had my head down on an important project." They will understand—they have important projects, too.

Create Deep Work Slices

You can't disappear into the deep work zone for several consecutive hours. But if you divide a deep work block into smaller segments, you can get more deep work done without sacrificing responsiveness.

Try to break the task at hand into mini milestones that you can accomplish in about 15 minutes. Set a timer and dive into the zone. Single-task until your mini milestone is complete or your 15 minutes has elapsed, then come up for air to check anything that needs to be checked. If you need to switch, do so. If not, set the next mini milestone and get back to deep work.

Track Your Distractions

Choose a day to track your multitasking down to the smallest detail. Keep a notepad nearby and write down everything that pulls you out of single-tasking.

Include work-related distractions (like email or noisy coworkers) and recreational distractions (like your favorite shopping website or the family group text). If something distracts you more than once, put a tick next to it each time. At the end of the day, look at your list. Rate each distraction from 1 to 3, with 1 being extremely distracting, 2 being somewhat distracting, and 3 being slightly distracting.

Yes, this step is tedious and time-consuming. But do it once and you'll glean two invaluable pieces of information: how much time you're losing to distraction and which distractions should be dealt with first.

Next, grab your list of distractions and notate it one more time. Write a "C" next to distractions within your control. Then write an "X" next to distractions that are not within your control. Now you're ready to make a distraction action plan. We'll create one in the next section.

Take Control of Distractions

You've identified your distractions, tracked their frequency, and noted whether they are within your control. Now it's time to reduce your distractions as much as possible. First, we'll explore how to reduce or eliminate the most common "C" distractions, or the ones you have control over, and reclaim your lost time. Then we'll tackle those "X" distractions, or the ones that are outside of your control.

How to Minimize Distractions You Can Control

The most powerful tool in reducing distraction is mindfulness. Because distraction is driven by our subconscious, we often don't realize we're distracted until we've already lost our focus. Practice maintaining a sense of awareness about where your attention is. Learn to notice when it has wandered and to recognize when the new focus is actually a distraction.

Eliminate digital clutter.
Each app, browser tab, and window not related to your immediate task is "digital clutter." The more digital clutter around you, the more likely you are to be distracted by technology. Close anything not related to your immediate task.

Email and instant messaging apps are particularly pernicious distractions. Avoid keeping these open. Instead, check them on a schedule. Closing and reopening your digital tools might seem annoying or time-consuming, but avoiding the distraction saves far more time and frustration in the long run.

Turn distractions into rewards or tasks.
When you recognize a distraction, don't indulge it. Log it. If the distraction is work-related, put it in your task manager. Don't spend too much time tracking down context right away. Just record the thought and get back to your main task. You can record additional context once your primary task is complete.

If it's a recreational distraction, like checking social media or reading an interesting article, make it a reward for completing a task. Once you've completed your task, allow yourself to enjoy that distraction guilt-free.

Silence your phone.
Social media, games, news, and other apps are designed to be addictive. Every time you fiddle with your apps, your brain releases a little bit of dopamine, the happy hormone. When the jolt dissipates, you remember it was your phone

that gave you that little moment of happiness and you're tempted to reach for it again.

Make it harder to get to those apps and for those apps to get to you. Don't keep your phone on your desk. Instead, put it in a drawer or leave it in your bag. If that's not possible, go in the settings for your most distracting apps and turn off their notifications.

Listen to your body.
Your brain's primary function is to keep your body alive. If your body doesn't have what it needs, you'll struggle to focus. If it seems like you're doing everything you can to stay focused but still failing, check in with your body. Mentally strenuous tasks are more challenging when you're hungry, thirsty, tired, or in need of the bathroom. Take a moment to give your body a boost instead of pushing through.

How to Handle Distractions You Can't Control

Despite your best efforts, there will always be distractions that are out of your control. But that doesn't mean you have to tolerate them outright. You can take steps to minimize their impact on your work product. Take a look at your distraction list again and note the things you marked as out of your control.

Interruptions from Coworkers
Colleagues rarely intend to make work harder for you. But interruptions, late requests, persistent messaging, and other disruptions do just that. Time Masters set and communicate boundaries that save them time while strengthening their professional relationships.

What kinds of boundaries reduce the impact of coworker interruptions?

Proactive steps, such as:

- Placing a sign on your desk or office door to indicate when disruptions are unwanted

- Setting a "Busy" or "Away" status on instant messaging apps

- Proactively communicating busy time to colleagues

- Wearing visible headphones

Reactive steps, such as:

- Inviting colleagues to come back at another time

- Proposing colleagues send their request via email

- Suggesting colleagues schedule a meeting

- Asking colleagues to quiet a noisy conversation or activity or move it elsewhere

You may worry that these actions are impolite, but each of them can be done tactfully. Give yourself permission to set limits. Understand what your ideal boundaries are and be ready to explain why you need them if someone asks.

Be willing to collaborate on a compromise if your preferences conflict with a key colleague's. Express appreciation when a colleague respects your boundaries and show respect when your colleagues express theirs.

Office Noise

Offices can be noisy places, but you don't have to endure acoustic chaos. Invest in a pair of high-quality noise-canceling headphones. If you can't move to a quieter place, white noise, nature sounds, music with no lyrics, or music you know well can block out office chatter without distracting you. Avoid unfamiliar music, music with interesting lyrics, or narrative works like podcasts or audiobooks. These will engage your language processing center and make your brain task-switch.

Experiment with different types of sounds. If you can't find something that works, try playing nothing at all. Simply wearing your headphones will reduce how much noise reaches you. It also has the added benefit of signaling to coworkers that you're busy and shouldn't be disturbed.

Your Emotional State

As much as you might wish you could, you can't control your thoughts and feelings. It's hard to focus when your emotions are charged, whether positively or negatively. But you can influence them. If your emotional state is distracting you, take a mindfulness break. Close your eyes and take a deep breath. Acknowledge your feelings and remind yourself what's important at this moment in time.

Send your thoughts to your SMART goals and remind yourself why the task at hand needs your attention. Remind yourself of your time management tools and invite your brain to refocus. Do this as many times as you need to get through the emotional flood.

Distraction management is both a habit and a skill. It takes practice to fill your toolbox with tools that work for you. If some don't, it's okay to set them aside and try something new.

You're not going to defeat distraction overnight. But keep taking proactive steps to reduce it by mindfully recognizing when you're distracted and redirecting yourself to your work. It will get easier and easier until it's second nature.

Tip: Tools to Reduce Distraction

There are many apps, programs, and extensions that can help us manage distraction. It's ironic, but sometimes the most effective solution to reducing technology's stranglehold on our attention is more technology.

Apple's Screen Time (iOS) and Google's Digital Wellbeing (Android) are mobile-only apps that track how much you use your phone. They show you how often you check your phone, how long your screen is active, and how much time you spend in certain apps. You can set time limits for apps you want to use less. Both are free and work on iOS and Android.

RescueTime automatically tracks your usage and provides you with a summary that shows how much time you spend on different apps and websites. Use the report to identify your distractions. Then use RescueTime's blocking function to keep you from visiting them when you should be working. It's available for desktop and mobile devices (iOS and Android) and has a yearly fee.

Identify Priorities

In chapter two, we started to explore 4Ns prioritization using importance and urgency as criteria. Remember, it's a classification system that provides you a useful shorthand to prioritize tasks and stay organized:

1. **Now:** High importance, high urgency

2. **Next:** High importance, low urgency

3. **Not by me (or not by myself):** Low importance, high urgency

4. **Never:** Low importance, low urgency

However, there will be times when you need more direction. What do you do if tasks have come from multiple sources? What if your "Now" list is overwhelmingly long? Your supervisor should be your top prioritization resource, and you should consult that person often. But you can't rely on your supervisor to reprioritize your to-do list multiple times a day. So what do you do when importance and urgency still don't give you enough clarity? Consider impact and resource intensity.

You've set SMART goals, and your company has key business objectives. How much impact does each task have on your goals and on your company's goals? Each task will take a certain amount of time and effort. You may have to invest other resources such as money, buy-in from others, or physical supplies. How resource-intensive is the task?

Focus on High-Value Activities

Tasks that have a big impact on your goals or your company's objectives are high-value activities. These activities deserve your time and attention because of their disproportionately large return on investment. If you focus on these activities first, you're far less likely to regret how you've spent your time—even if you can't get to tasks further down the list. Here's how to tackle high-value activities.

Assess a high-value task's resource intensity. Not all your high-value activities will have the same resource intensity. Some will be more complex and demand more from you or your team. These "tasks" are more like projects. Make sure to check in with your supervisors and any other stakeholders about tasks that are high impact but resource-intensive.

Ensure tasks are completable and have stakeholder buy-in. Do not work on resource-intensive tasks until you are sure you have buy-in from all relevant stakeholders. Otherwise, you risk expending effort on a project that fizzles out midway through execution. If you can't get buy-in, the project should no longer be considered high-value.

Break complex projects down into achievable tasks. Once you have buy-in on a complex project, break it into smaller tasks so it doesn't feel overwhelming.

Communicate with stakeholders. Keep the lines of communication open to make sure everyone is on the same page. Most importantly, ask for help if you hit snags. Struggling to complete a task with insufficient resources is a waste of time.

Remember Mitch, our teaching assistant from chapter two? His high-value activities included grading papers, doing research, and tutoring students. Prioritizing these tasks means he gets his most important work done first.

Grading papers and tutoring students are high-value tasks, but they aren't usually complex or difficult. He is already an expert in the subjects he's helping his students learn. He just has to put in the time.

However, his research is much more mentally demanding, will take more time, and has many more pieces. He's also dependent on other people to achieve his research goals, such as other graduate students, his study participants, or his advisor. He should always be looking for ways to make his research more efficient without sacrificing its quality.

Delegate or Back-Burner Low-Value Activities

You may be assigned tasks that have a low impact on your goals. Often, these low-value tasks should be avoided, but sometimes they are worth completing. Low-value doesn't mean no value. Here's how to tackle low-value activities.

Assess a low-value task's resource intensity. If these low-value tasks are also low-resource, you can knock them out quickly. This can be an energizing way to stack wins and build momentum. But be mindful, the resources you expend on low-value activities still add up. You will eventually reach a tipping point where your efforts would be better spent elsewhere.

Reassess any low-value, high-intensity tasks. If a low-value task has high resource intensity, take steps to get out of doing it. Talk to relevant stakeholders and make sure they understand the complexity of the task they've requested. Someone who isn't familiar with your job might not realize what they've asked for. Checking in gives them the opportunity to adjust or withdraw the task. This builds trust and credibility.

Communicate with stakeholders. Ask questions to clarify the purpose of the task. You may have limited context on where the task fits into your company's overall objectives. Getting more information about its value may prompt you to reprioritize it upward and get started more quickly. While these conversations may feel like they are slowing you down, they're actually investments in your time. The more information you have about the context of your assigned tasks, the more accurately you'll prioritize them, and the more efficiently you'll get them done.

Ariel, the professor Mitch assists in chapter two, has excellent time management. One of the ways she manages her time is by delegating to Mitch tasks that are of low value to her as an influential political science scholar. Sometimes these tasks are tedious, administrative, and not very high value to Mitch, either. But as Mitch doesn't have the option of delegating them to someone else, he needs to prioritize them after his grading, tutoring, and research work. Mitch and Ariel's communication about the value of tasks is critical so he has all the context necessary to get the tasks done at the right time.

Leverage Your Knowledge into a Plan

Each task should now have four characteristics categorized: importance, urgency, impact, and resource intensity. You're ready to start scheduling your tasks. Communication remains key. You don't work in isolation. Each task has stakeholders depending on you to turn in a high-quality work product on time. Check in when you hit milestones to see if the context has changed.

It's particularly important to stay on the same page with people who have requested tasks that you've assigned a low priority. They are a low priority to you but a high priority to them. They should know when to expect the final deliverable or get an update about its progress. Maintaining stakeholder alignment builds trust and protects your professional reputation.

Using this prioritization matrix to create your work plan gives you clarity and direction. In the beginning, you may want to note each of these criteria in your task manager. But as you seek out the necessary information and make ongoing assessments, this prioritization will become automatic. Over time, you won't need to notate as explicitly.

Myles, our user experience designer from the beginning of this chapter, isn't going to be able to stop saying yes overnight. It's going to take a while for him to get comfortable declining irrelevant requests from his colleagues. But by making a habit of proactively communicating and regularly reprioritizing, he can start to turn his seemingly endless to-do list into a work plan. He'll begin to notice what kinds of tasks consistently end up at the bottom of the list, and it'll become easier to say no when an irrelevant, low-value request comes in.

FOUR

Your Secret Weapon: The Contingency Plan

Improvisation has played a starring role in the creation of many of humanity's greatest inventions, from sticky notes to penicillin. We've also relied on our capacity to use the past to predict the future to drive civilization's advancement from agriculture to spaceflight. But it's when we combine the two—inventiveness and intention—that we make our most considerable strides in growth, innovation, and success.

"Thrown Off Guard on Thursday"

In her 10 years as a social worker, Mel has helped thousands of families, but she keeps seeing the same pattern. Parents who struggle to keep their families happy and healthy are always missing two things: skills and support. She believes her agency could be more proactive in getting parents what they needed to be successful. She knows she can help them avoid ending up in the kinds of situations that have social workers like her knocking on their doors.

She writes up a proposal for a workshop series for new parents and presents it to her director, Robert. Three weeks later, she has a green light for eight workshops, 20 hours from the marketing team, and $12,000. She couldn't be more excited. It's time to get started.

Her first progress report is full of successes. She has a great speaker to teach the parents about managing stress. The local community center is available on her preferred date and has plenty of room for the 50 couples she hopes to host. The catering comes in under budget and offers a nonprofit discount. All she needs is attendees.

That's when things start to fall apart.

Vince, the marketing assistant assigned to her initiative, is clearly overwhelmed. His deliverables fall further and further behind schedule. By the time the campaign is ready to start, the workshop is only 10 days away. She is able to get 41 couples to RSVP, but only 16 actually come.

She's so busy cringing at the empty chairs that she jumps when the speaker taps her on the shoulder. The internet isn't working, and the speaker can't access her presentation. The event is supposed to start in 10 minutes.

She tries to find someone in the administrative office to help, but the lights are off. The center's coordinator left shortly after letting Mel in. She apologizes to the speaker, but there is nothing she can do about the internet.

The speaker presses on without a presentation, and Mel turns her attention to the catering, which is late. When it finally arrives, Mel watches in horror as they put out food for 60 couples when there are only 16 in the next room. She never updated the count.

She hears applause signaling the workshop has ended and heads back into the main room. It's time for the networking session. She thanks everyone for coming and directs them to the excessively large feast. She mingles, encouraging the parents to enjoy the food and talk to each other. She greets a mother who asks why none of the food options are vegetarian. She apologizes profusely, mentally kicking herself. How did she not think of that?

As the event comes to a close, she collects the comment cards and encourages parents to take home as much food as they can carry. She flips through the cards and grimaces. The positive feedback is tepid, at best.

Most of the cards express disappointment. They call the event disorganized, awkward, and unprofessional. If she is being honest, she can't blame them.

Robert is not going to be happy.

This situation illustrates an important point applicable for anyone facing a big project. Some tasks are best done with the creativity and ingenuity that comes from winging it. Others benefit from the structure of planning. But your most important tasks need a bit of both—especially when things go wrong. It's easy to panic when faced with a huge gap between reality and your plans. But you can still hit a home run when life throws curveballs. The way to succeed in the face of obstacles is through contingency planning.

Creating Your Workflow Contingency Plan

Contingency planning isn't just for earthquakes and spy missions. It's also useful for ordinary problems, such as when a key person in your presentation team gets sick, a technical failure like downed Wi-Fi happens, or someone forgets the snacks. Time Masters make contingency planning a regular part of the way they work, so obstacles cost them as little time as possible. An easy way to visualize this type of planning is with a contingency tree, which allows you to track each possible problem and your response. We'll walk through creating one later in the chapter.

Contingency planning is simple: Brainstorm ways your plans could fail, and then identify what you'll do if those obstacles appear. Contingency planning is neither pessimistic nor optimistic. It's realistic. Life has too many variables for your plans to go smoothly every time. Preparing for possible snags gives your plans the flexibility to succeed even in a challenging context.

Identify Potential Points of Failure

The first step of contingency planning is risk assessment. That's because every task or project depends on particular prerequisites for success. Sometimes these prerequisites are simple. Emptying your email inbox only requires a functioning device, internet connectivity, a password, and a little time. But bigger, more complex projects, such as throwing an event, have longer, more elaborate prerequisites. You might need to give a presentation for that event, provide catering, or produce a video to be shown at it. Each prerequisite is a potential point of failure.

Not all of the prerequisites for every task or program carry the same weight. Some critical prerequisites could have a huge impact on your operation, while others are minor. For example, having Wi-Fi for an interactive presentation to the corporate leaders is a big prerequisite. Downed internet would cause complete chaos. But if one of the head honchos is late, it's easier to work around.

In this step, identify as many instances you can think of where things could go wrong. Consider how these potential points of failure could endanger your ability to complete your project well and on time. Be as expansive as possible in this step.

Avoid the urge to evaluate your ideas. You'll do that later. It's better to narrow down from many possibilities than to edit yourself prematurely and miss something vital.

I know it's challenging to think about all the things that can go wrong for an event that you're excited about. When I talk about this issue with my clients, I present them with this checklist; a jumping-off point to get you going. Once you get the hang of it, the list will become second nature.

Time

- Must it be completed by a specific date or time?

- Are there any milestones that must be finished on time to stay on track?

- Are there any components that could take significantly longer than expected?

Cost

- Do you need to acquire or stick to a specific budget?

- Is there a process for getting access to your funds?
- Are there any components that could cost more than expected?

Stakeholders

- Do you need deliverables from others?
- Do you need approval from others?
- Do you need participation from others?

Resources

- Do you require materials or equipment?
- Does anything need to be delivered to a physical place?
- Are you going to be working with external vendors?

Environmental

- Is your task or project weather dependent?
- Can local events impact your success?
- Can national events affect your success?

Technical

- Do you need internet connectivity?
- Do you need audio/visual capabilities?
- Do you need access to special expertise to set up or operate equipment?

As you identify your prerequisites, you may get over-whelmed by all the things that could go wrong. Remember, you're not brainstorming these potential points of failure because you believe something terrible will happen. You are setting yourself up to be ready in case disaster strikes.

Prioritize Your Risks

Now that you've identified your potential points of failure, it's time to figure out which to plan for. Prioritizing your risks sets you up to spend the right amount of time preparing for the right amount of risk.

I like the efficiency of this impact/probability matrix to help figure out what can go wrong and where to focus your attention. Plotting your risks to a matrix helps you identify which deserve advanced planning and which are better left to improvisation in the moment. You'll realize that some tasks are essential to your success and deserve to be at the top of your list.

Rate each potential point of failure. Which are most likely and which are most impactful?

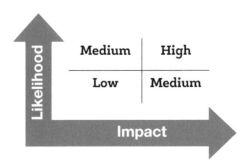

Once you've plotted each of your potential points of failure, it's time to consider precisely how much contingency planning is useful for the task at hand. For more straightforward tasks or projects, you may only spend a few minutes thinking over what you'd do about your very highest-risk concerns. More involved tasks might need multiple meetings, pages of documents, and buy-in from many stakeholders. A multimillion-dollar construction project deserves detailed contingency planning because of its cost, complexity, and stakes. But a simple client presentation may only need a quick conversation with a colleague.

It can be tempting—especially for perfectionists—to plan for every risk you've identified. But there's a tipping point where contingency planning stops being useful and starts being a distraction. Plan for medium- and low-risk concerns only if the project really deserves it.

Get Stakeholders on Board

Contingency planning is not as common as it should be. When a project gets the green light, colleagues and other stakeholders are often excited to start. But they may hesitate to pause for necessary contingency planning because of the extra work involved, because it may be considered a waste of time, because it may seem pessimistic, or because they think it may bring bad luck.

Since contingency planning is important, you need to be prepared to make the case for it. Start by explaining the need. It's just not realistic for every event, meeting, or presentation to go just as we imagined, so ensuring that your team has backup plans is key. This could be as simple as bringing a second set of cords for the laptop to plug into a projector. Or it could mean making the facility manager at the event center aware of your need for extra chairs for last-minute attendees. Emphasize that your goal is to make sure you and the team are prepared and set up for success, not to create more work or be a killjoy. Be clear about what you are asking people for. Set an expectation of time and resources that people will need to devote to contingency planning. Make sure they understand how this process benefits them.

Lead by example by doing as much of the heavy lifting as you can ahead of time. Assemble your initial thoughts into an email or document to share with stakeholders and invite them to collaborate with you. Ask them to help you make the contingency plan stronger to save you all time, effort, and frustration.

Draft Your Plan

You've identified your risks, prioritized them, and gotten stakeholders on board with the contingency planning process. It's time to draft your plan. Your contingency plan has three parts: risks, triggers, and responses.

As you write your plan—whether it's an in-depth proposal, a thoughtful email, or a quick instant message—make sure you keep the person to whom you are writing in mind. Don't assume that person has the same background information that you do. Someone on your team might be able to read between the lines, but your supervisor or a person on a different team might need more context. Include all the necessary context for anyone who might need to use it.

Be specific about what circumstances mean a risk has become a reality and when it's time to respond. Define your trigger ahead of time when you're calm and level-headed. This is particularly helpful for high-pressure situations or when lots of people are involved. When you or your team are stressed, you may be too eager or too hesitant to respond to an issue as it unfolds.

For example, if your project requires sunny weather, do you trigger your contingency plan as soon as rain is forecast? Or do you wait for the sky to fill with clouds? If a storm threatens, you won't waste time negotiating when to take action because your plan will lay the groundwork for when and where actions take place.

Once you've identified the trigger, outline the response. How will you cope with the problem? Do you need to change your expectations for what success looks like? Do you need to call in additional resources? Do you need to communicate with someone? Document and communicate your planned response as needed.

Next, identify any resources or stakeholders that need to be assembled ahead of time for your contingency plan to work. Make sure they are available now and will be available when you need them. For example, if your contingency plan calls for extra staffers, make sure you know how to activate them, and—importantly—that they are ready to jump in if you need them.

Lastly, assess if any of your risks can be avoided, managed, or shared. Contingency planning's biggest benefit is that it helps you understand if you can reduce a risk's likelihood or impact.

I put these into three categories:

- Avoid Risk: Steps to avoid risk might include bringing additional equipment or updating an old software system.

- Share Risk: Steps to share risk might include getting insurance or negotiating a cancellation policy.

- Manage Risk: Steps to manage risk might include bringing along a case of ponchos or printing extra copies of a handout.

It's impossible to mitigate all of the risk, so you'll still need your contingency plan. But taking a few proactive steps will reduce how likely you are to need it.

Lastly, remember that your contingency plan is only useful when it's up to date. If you're working on a longer-term initiative, set a time to review and revise it. If you incorporate new information or make changes, ensure all stakeholders have access to the up-to-date version. Track down old versions and delete them.

Create a Contingency Tree

Now that you know the process, let's walk through an example. Mel, our social worker, was so excited to flex her entrepreneurial muscles with a workshop series for new parents. But nothing went to plan at her first event. What would it look like if she did some contingency planning before starting on the second one?

While there are eight workshops in Mel's series, the individual events are essentially the same. She gets attendees to come to the community center to learn from an expert. Afterward, they connect with each other while enjoying light snacks. What should Mel's contingency plan look like? A contingency tree can help her visualize what problems are likely and how she can respond to them.

Mel's Contingency Tree

The first branches in a contingency tree are the prerequisites for success. What are Mel's prerequisites?

- A suitable venue

- Functional equipment

- A qualified speaker

- Sufficient catering

- Adequate attendance

- Attendee satisfaction

- Coming in under budget

Each of these is a potential point of failure, and we saw some of the ways they could go wrong with her first workshop. Mel's second set of branches would include the problem she encountered in her first event.

- She was able to book the community center, but its internet wasn't working on the day of the event.

- Her catering came in under budget, but she ended up with too much food and no vegetarian options.

- She missed her RSVP goal because of delays in her marketing efforts.

- Because there were so many snags, many of the attendees were unhappy with the experience.

Mel could have anticipated all of these issues with some contingency planning. As she starts working on her second workshop, what are some additional risks she should consider planning for?

- What if the venue cancels?

- What if it's missing the necessary technology or equipment?

- What if the speaker cancels?

- What if the catering arrives but is incorrect or low quality?

- What if the marketing materials are low quality or ineffective?

- What if her costs exceed her budget?

- What if there's inclement weather on the day of the event?

She then needs to decide which risks are the biggest threats to her workshops.

When she considers the impact and likelihood, a few stand out as needing serious consideration. Issues with her venue are very high impact, but the likelihood is on the lower side. Problems with her marketing are both high impact and high likelihood. Though losing her speaker is of the lowest likelihood, it would force her to cancel the workshop. Each of these should be incorporated into her level two branches.

Next, she needs to get stakeholders on board with her contingency planning effort. Given the issues with the first event, her desire to plan ahead will likely be well received by her boss, Robert. But she might have to do more work to get Vince, the marketing coordinator, on board. He might feel that the planning is retaliation for his late deliverables or that it's more work he doesn't have time for. She'll be able to get over his objections if she focuses on their mutual goal for a successful event and does much of the planning herself.

Now it's time for Mel to make her plan. Her resources are limited, her event is relatively simple, and her timeline is tight. It doesn't make sense to have a detailed plan for every single contingency. She chooses to focus on her venue, marketing, and speakers. For each risk, she needs to decide when to avoid, manage, share, or respond.

For her venue, she decides to avoid the risk of equipment issues. She makes a note to call the community center on the morning of the event. If they don't have the correct number of tables and chairs ready, she knows which rental company to hire. She'll manage the risk of internet issues by using some of her budget to purchase a Wi-Fi hot spot device. She'll respond to a venue cancellation by moving the workshop online.

She works through each of her high-risk factors, noting her plans in the level three branches of her contingency tree. Once all of her thoughts are organized, she shares the tree with Robert and Vince and asks for their feedback. They come up with a few ideas that she incorporates into the final version of the contingency tree. They expand the tree into a simple one-page document outlining the risks, their triggers, and their responses.

Workshop two isn't perfect. The marketing is nearly late again, but Mel simplifies her request so the campaign can start on time. She even hits her RSVP goal six days before the deadline. Every seat is filled, and the speaker gives an excellent presentation. The attendees barely notice when the community center's Wi-Fi goes down again. Because Mel set up the hot spot ahead of time, the speaker's computer automatically switches to the functioning network. When she reviews the comment cards, they're full of compliments.

The next day, she meets with Robert and Vince to review. They celebrate what worked and update the contingency plan to account for what didn't. By investing a few hours into contingency planning, Mel delivered a higher-quality work product while saving time, money, energy, and frustration.

Risk Assessment

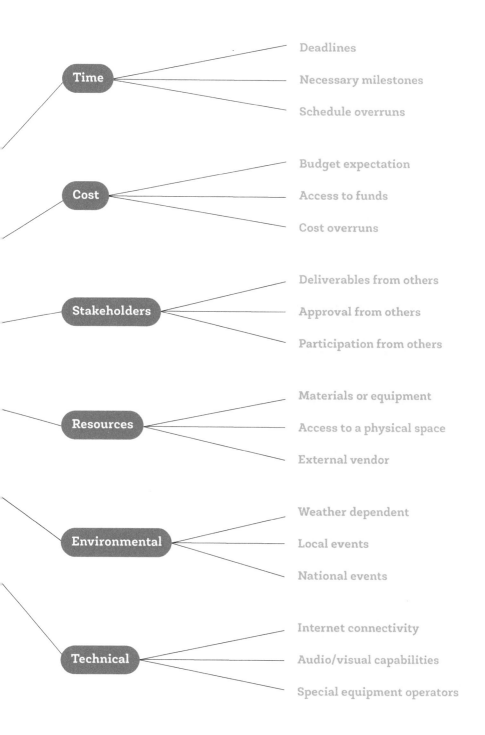

Time
- Deadlines
- Necessary milestones
- Schedule overruns

Cost
- Budget expectation
- Access to funds
- Cost overruns

Stakeholders
- Deliverables from others
- Approval from others
- Participation from others

Resources
- Materials or equipment
- Access to a physical space
- External vendor

Environmental
- Weather dependent
- Local events
- National events

Technical
- Internet connectivity
- Audio/visual capabilities
- Special equipment operators

Now It's Your Turn

The workday starts with the best of intentions but rarely goes to plan. Contingency planning can save you time at work. Let's start by creating a contingency tree you can start using tomorrow: one for your average workday. Use the space on these two pages to map out your plan.

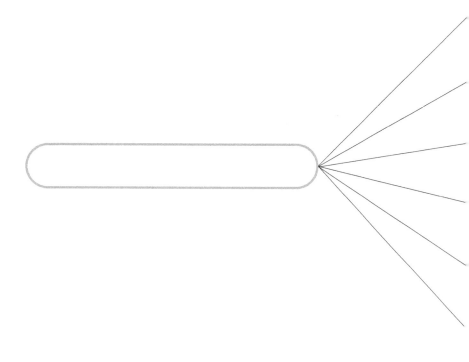

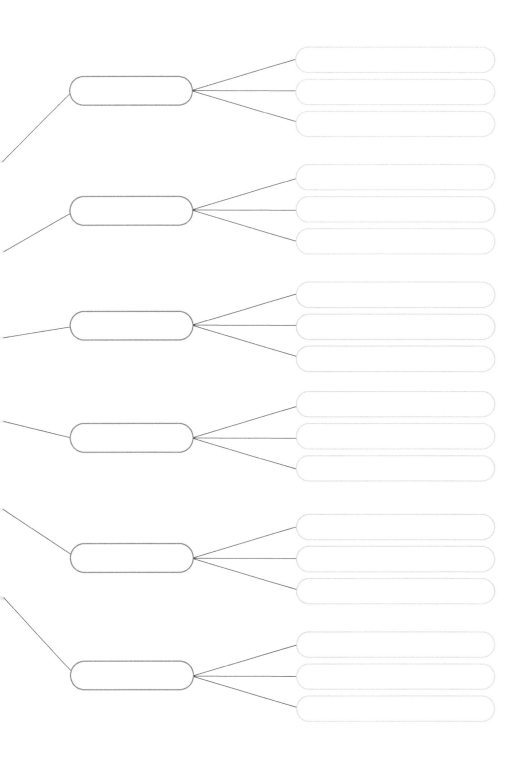

CREATE YOUR BRANCHES:

Grab a notebook and think through each of the following questions to identify your workday's potential points of failure. You may end up with a big list of potential points of failure. But don't be overwhelmed by it. You want to be expansive at this stage and refine later.

Time

- Do you have to work particular hours?

- What kind of deadlines do you usually have?

- How many meetings do you usually have?

- Is there work that must be completed same-day or faster?

- Are there any work products that could take significantly longer than expected?

Costs

- Does your work require managing or acquiring a budget?

- Is there a process for getting access to those funds?

- Are there any components that have unpredictable costs?

- Is the budget generally sufficient for you to get your work done well and on time?

- What happens if you can't get the funds you need?

Stakeholders

- Do you need deliverables, approval, or participation from others?

- Are those people internal or external to your organization?

- Are there specific people who can complicate your day?

- Is your work directly impacted by the activities of your company's competitors?

- Are you a stakeholder in anyone else's work?

Resources

- What materials or supplies do you need?

- What equipment do you use regularly?

- Will you be working with external vendors?

- Do you provide resources to anyone else?

Environmental Factors

- Does your work need to be done in a specific location?

- Is your work affected by the weather?

- Are there disruptive elements (e.g., noise, interruptions from colleagues)?

- Does your work change based on the time of year (e.g., back-to-school season or tax time)?

- Can your work be affected by what's happening in the news (e.g., an election or a celebrity wedding)?

- Can it be impacted by what's happening in your local area (e.g., a parade or a convention)?

Technical Details

- Do you need internet connectivity?

- Do you need specific skills to use your technology, tools, or equipment?

- Do you have all the technology you need to do your work?

- Is your technical equipment of good quality and in good working order?

- Who is responsible for providing or maintaining your equipment?

You may have a big list of potential points of failure. Don't be overwhelmed by it. Stay focused on your goal of creating a contingency plan that saves you time if things go wrong.

Now that you've identified your potential points of failure, it's time to figure out which to plan for. Here's how to come up with your plan.

Prioritize your risks. This sets you up to spend the right amount of time preparing for the right amount of risk.

Rate each potential point of failure using your impact/probability matrix. Which are most likely and which are most impactful? Which risks are problematic enough to deserve an up-front investment of planning time?

Identify the stakeholders in your work. Would it be useful if they were included in your contingency planning process? If so, let them know that you want to use contingency planning to transform how you manage your workday. Explain how it can help you be more efficient, effective, and consistent. Ensure they know that you'll be putting the plan together but that you'd like their ideas, support, and feedback.

Write down your plan. What should your plan look like, and where should it live? Don't let your contingency plan remain a mental exercise. Even a sticky note taped to your desk is better than relying on memory. Depending on the complexity of your work, you may need more than that. If you need to share it with others, include all the context they will need.

Gather your resources. Ensure that you have everything you need to put your contingency plan into action as soon as a trigger is tripped. If noise is a risk and your plan is to pop on a pair of headphones, you don't want to be stuck without them.

Take steps to mitigate your risks. Avoiding, managing, or sharing risk usually saves time.

Set a time in the future to revisit your plan. Be prepared to update it if necessary.

Coping with the Unexpected

You can do your best to plan for problems. You can do your best to be proactive about preventing them. But ultimately, you can't predict the future. Things can go wrong in ways you didn't expect. This doesn't mean you didn't do a good job preparing or planning. It just means that, despite your best efforts, life remains unpredictable.

I can confidently say that in 2019, almost no one included "pandemic" in their contingency plans. Yet in 2020, we each found ourselves forced to respond to a crisis we'd never imagined. Everyone's way of living and working was thrown into flux. We each had to decide what to fight to preserve, what to change, and what to give up on.

When the unexpected happens—and it will happen—you get to decide how you will respond. You can panic, but that's probably not the best use of the finite time you have. When should you push through? When should you ask for help? When should you adjust your expectations or goals? When should you call it a wash and move on? Let's explore ways to respond to unexpected setbacks and obstacles.

Last-Ditch Effort

While unexpected, some problems aren't severe enough to threaten your ability to get things done well and on time. If you pause to regroup and adjust, it's possible to get back to work. But other setbacks are so severe, they threaten to derail everything. How you react to emergencies can be the difference between an astonishing success and a catastrophic failure.

Your instinct might be to go into crisis mode. But the last thing you want to do is let an emotional reaction to anxiety or pressure control you. Take a deep breath, reject crisis mode, go into crisis *reaction* mode, and calmly respond to the problem.

The first order of business is to decide whether you should dig in or dig out. If your goal is still achievable, you may want to adapt and persevere. For example, in 2020 the service and restaurant industries were hit hard by the shutdowns governments mandated in response to the coronavirus pandemic. Unfortunately, many didn't survive. Those that did can teach us lessons about how to be creative, resilient, and wise in the face of unexpected obstacles.

Adapting requires stepping back from the how and focusing on the why. What are you trying to accomplish, and why? Restaurants need to sell meals. Trainers need to sell personal fitness services. They need to sell their products to stay in business. Ideally, these activities happen in a dining room or a gym. But some savvy business owners realized their goals could be accomplished in a different way or in a different context.

Resourceful restaurants sought to make takeout and delivery easier by investing in new technology. Some restaurants offered virtual cooking lessons. Creative trainers offered online and outdoor classes. Instead of panicking, they adapted.

When an unexpected problem sends your plan into crisis, think about the ultimate objective of your task. Ask yourself these questions:

- Can you get it done if you're given more resources (e.g., time, money, people power)?

- Can anything in your contingency plan be adapted to address this problem?

- Is the problem inherently temporary, and will it resolve on its own with time?

If the answer to these questions is yes, then dig in. With a little perseverance, you can get back on track. If the answer is no, consider these questions:

- Is there another way to reach the ultimate objective of this task?

- Is it possible to change the definition of success?

- Is there a different outcome that could be considered "good enough"?

If the answer to these questions is also no, your focus should be on digging out. But if the answer to these questions is yes, dig in though with some adaptations. You can still accomplish your goal, but you'll have to change your approach to get there.

Could Mel get her workshop series back on track if the coronavirus pandemic threatened her success?

More resources wouldn't have kept the governor from shutting down her venue. They wouldn't have made her speakers or attendees more willing to gamble with their health by attending in person. Pursuing more time, money, or staff would have been a waste. Ultimately, she would have ended up with no event at all.

However, she did have a last-minute venue cancellation in her contingency plan. In that case, Mel planned to use videoconferencing software. Many in the education industry quickly responded to government shutdowns of meeting spaces by doing the same. But this solution only addressed half of her workshops' ultimate objective.

Presenting via webinar would teach skills to new parents. But it wouldn't help them connect with each other and create a community of support. She would need to adapt further.

Mel could use social media to set up an online support community for the new parents. This isn't what she envisioned. But, under the circumstances, it would make sense for her to redefine success here. She could set a new goal: Get 50 percent of the attendees to join the online community.

Though a change from her original plan, it would still serve her underlying goal as well as her agency's: helping new parents thrive. By taking time to evaluate and adapt her approach, Mel would save time in execution and still get to a good outcome.

Tip: Communicating with Stakeholders if You Need to Hit the Reset Button

When setbacks derail your plans, you might feel embarrassed, anxious, or stressed. Resist the urge to try to fix the problem in secret. This can backfire. Instead, proactively communicate with stakeholders. This will make you look trustworthy, conscientious, and competent.

Here's an outline you can use to communicate with confidence:

Show that you prepared: Show stakeholders how you set up the project for success to communicate that you did everything you could to prevent the setback.

Explain the cause and effect clearly: Be concise, but consider your audience. Don't expect stakeholders to read between the lines.

Present your response plan: Outline how you plan to react to the crisis and why you believe it will be effective.

Get stakeholders on board: Tie your plan to the key objectives at stake.

Ask for feedback: Demonstrate that you are open to ideas on how to improve your approach or prevent future setbacks.

Acceptance and Moving On

We can all think of a situation we stuck with for too long. It might have been a doomed relationship, a dead-end job, or a miserable living situation. In retrospect, we can usually identify the tipping point where we should have called it quits. What do we lament most of all? The wasted time.

This is a mistake that psychologists call the sunk cost fallacy. Instead of recognizing the situation for what it is, we focus on what we wish it was and how much we've already invested in it. This biases us toward investing more resources instead of recognizing a failure as such. The sunk cost fallacy causes unimaginable damage to human happiness and potential.

Some industries were able to use creativity and grit to succeed within the 2020 pandemic's constraints. Others were forced to abandon their plans. The entertainment industry couldn't operate safely and had to shut down for months. Studios had to delay television and movie productions indefinitely. Many theaters, concert halls, sports leagues, and arenas canceled entire seasons. They had to accept that there was no way to push forward despite billions in sunk cost.

The next crisis you face may not be as inescapable as a pandemic. What should you do when the situation is dire but perseverance is still possible? Just because digging in is an option doesn't mean it's the right one. You might chafe at the idea of admitting defeat. You might still hold on to hope that your luck might turn for the better.

You might hate the idea of having wasted all the effort you've already put in. This is the sunk cost fallacy rearing its ugly head. You don't have time to waste on it.

- Ditch optimism for realism and be honest about the likelihood of success.

- Calculate the cost of perseverance and compare it to the probability of success.

- Develop a realistic appraisal of what success can look like under your circumstances.

- Decide if the cost is worth the potential gain despite the risk.

There's a point where the likelihood or value of success is so low that investing additional resources is a waste. If you're going to lose resources failing, it's better to lose as few as possible. Shift your mindset from perseverance and adaptation to acceptance and learning. Making this change is as simple as asking a new question.

Instead of asking, "What do I do now?" ask, "What do I do next?"

- Was the crisis predictable?

- Was it preventable?

- Could it have been mitigated in some way?

- Given what you know now, is there anything you would have done differently?

- Is there something you can do in the future to make the crisis less likely to happen again?

- Is another occurrence likely enough that you should take those steps?

When a crisis has taken hold and there's no way to recover, the goal becomes emerging stronger and wiser. Accept that things fell apart, but don't wallow in regret. Learn from the experience without beating yourself up or pointing fingers.

FIVE

Inside Out

Your time management toolbox is full. It's time to start building. You're ready to create a productivity system that will keep you organized, prioritized, and focused—a system that will turn you into a Time Master. You might be overwhelmed by all the options. Perhaps you feel intimidated by how much change is necessary or you're unsure where to begin. That's normal. Don't let it hold you back from starting on this more efficient method of time management. I promise the results are worth it.

While every successful time management system is different, they have four traits in common: They're effective, scalable, flexible, and sustainable. In this chapter, we'll explore how to build a system with these traits that is customized for you.

"Finally Focusing on Friday"

Let's revisit the people who opened each of the chapters in this book—Chelsea, Mitch, Myles, and Mel—and see how they're faring now that they've taken steps to improve their time management.

Chelsea

Chelsea checks her notes one last time as Greg settles into his seat. It's been a month since her disastrous performance review, and she is excited to update him. She had promised him that she would fix her time management issues, and she's made progress.

Some changes were simple. She modified her notification settings, which solved her tardiness problem. Instead of pinging her at the start time of a meeting, Chelsea set the reminder for 10 minutes before. She hasn't been late again since.

Improving her accuracy has been a harder nut to crack, but she is making strides. She's started asking Jesse, another team member, to proofread her deliverables before she submits them. She was worried about bothering him, so she offered to return the favor. Their proofreading trades have become a regular practice that improves both their work and their relationship.

Mitch

Mitch is excited for his weekly check-in meeting with Ariel. Since he gave up his shabby planner and started using the apps that Ariel recommended, he hasn't missed a class or work appointment.

He still keeps his paper journal handy, but only for short-term note-taking. The time he forgot his notebook at home, it didn't cause a crisis. And he no longer needs to cross things out or rewrite when updating a task or an appointment.

Most importantly, he can finally see everything at a glance. While he still has a lot to do, organizing it all feels easy and updating is a manageable task. That wall of accolades in Ariel's office no longer feels out of reach.

Myles

After the embarrassing planning meeting, Myles asks Cece if they can talk through everything on his plate. He knows that some of his tasks are outside of the scope of his role, but he isn't sure how to get out of doing them.

Cece starts by restating the company's goals, how the user experience team fits into them, and why his job is important. As they go through his to-do list, Myles is shocked. So much of what he's taken on is irrelevant to his work—and he hadn't even realized it.

Cece reiterates the point she made after the planning meeting disaster. "Focus on your job. Prioritize your work first. It's okay for other people's stuff to wait. If anyone has a problem with that, they can talk to me."

Myles hasn't quite perfected saying "no." But he's getting better at saying "not now."

Mel

Mel gives herself a mental pat on the back as she says goodbye to the final guest. Workshop six is complete, and she feels like a pro. Her secret weapon—the contingency "what-if doc"—has saved her yet again. This time, the caterer canceled at the last minute because of a power outage. Mel ordered pizzas, and the guests never noticed.

The universe always seemed to find a way to throw something new at her. But with her contingency plan, she was unstoppable. And with so many events under her belt, she is full of tricks to get a workshop back on track.

Still, she is surprised when Robert asks her to plan a new workshop for a new audience: teaching her colleagues how to pull off seamless events.

Time to Reassess

I often encounter overeager clients who are so excited to get to work and see results right away that they want to skip this clarity step. These clients have the most challenging journeys and are the most likely to give up before reaching their goal. They frequently struggle with focus and bounce impatiently from technique to technique. They sometimes take on too much change too quickly, then burn out and give up. Typically they work on the wrong problems and wonder why they aren't generating the results they want. But all of this is preventable.

The clients who get the best results in the least amount of time are willing to reflect. They take whatever time they need to get crystal clear on the why, what, and how. Over the last four chapters, you've learned about why particular challenges are common and what techniques are helpful. You may have even started implementing some of them. But as you begin to build your system, take some time to get clarity on your situation. This step ensures all your efforts will be pointed in the right direction.

Reconnect with Your Deep Why

You may have noticed a theme of perseverance throughout this book. Change is hard. It takes effort, and the path from struggle to success is rarely a straight line. This is why it's so important to get clarity on the real purpose of your journey. When you understand your reasons for wanting to improve your time management skills, you have a better chance of succeeding.

Think back to how you got through the most difficult challenges in your life. Either you didn't have a choice but to push through, or you had a very good reason to fight for a better future. You can choose to manage your time as you always have. You might be able to muddle along or find a new job if your productivity issues land you in hot water. But that's a miserable existence, and you wouldn't have picked up this book if you wanted that.

You have a good reason to do the hard work of transforming your time management. You discovered it in the Deep Whys exercise in chapter one. Review your answers from before. Do they still resonate with you? Based on what you've learned, do you need to adjust them?

1. Describe what is happening.

2. Describe how it's impacting you.

3. Describe why you want to change the situation.

4. Put these together into a sentence that describes your Deep Why.

Keep your Deep Whys in your mind as you build your system and put it in place. Call back to them often to generate motivation, whether things are going smoothly or you're hitting a rough patch.

Give It Presence

I encourage you to find a way to make your Deep Why physically present in your life. What I mean is find an image, a mantra, or an object to represent the reason of your Deep Why and place it on or around your desk so you can see it daily. I had one client whose Deep Why was tied to her financial success. She made a motivation board from images cut out from magazines. Each represented an aspect of what her life would look like when she met her goals. She put the board on a wall in her office and touched it every day.

The Deep Why for another client was tied to making time for his family. He decided to choose a comic book hero with super speed as a mascot to help him stay focused on this goal. He put an action figure of this mascot on his desk next to a picture of him playing with his children. The action figure and the photo served as constant reminders that efficiency keeps him from missing moments with his kids.

Your Deep Why symbol or ritual doesn't have to be complicated. It could be as simple as writing down your sentence each morning in a journal. That daily reminder is a powerful touchstone to get you centered and ready to go—even when times get tough.

Prioritize Your Challenges

Your time management challenges aren't simple. If they were, you'd have solved them already. They're a big, hairy, complex problem. The list of things to improve may be long. The issues might magnify each other. The whole mess is intimidating and overwhelming. Working on all of them at the same time is impossible. But if you prioritize them and resolve the most impactful ones first, you'll steadily dismantle the problem.

In the Writing It All Down activity from chapter one, you reflected on the time management issues you'd encountered in the previous week. Go back to your notes and rank each on how frequently it happens and how impactful it is. With your newly ordered list in hand, see if you notice any underlying patterns. Are several of your top-ranked issues tied to distraction? Disorganization? Lack of priori-tization? Something else? If so, that theme should be your first focus.

This means you'll have to allow some of the challenges on your list to remain unresolved in the short term. For some people, the idea of leaving some things broken might feel stressful. Take comfort that the dynamic that makes problems amplify each other also works in reverse. As you resolve your top-priority issues, you'll start to notice your lower-priority issues lessening as well.

One client, Julia, wanted to reduce how much she procrastinated. She used time blocking to give structure to her day and make it easier to start tasks. Her procrasti-nation improved, and she noticed that she was getting her work done faster and with fewer errors. She also noticed that she seemed to succumb to distraction less frequently. She worked on procrastination but unwittingly improved her accuracy, speed, and focus because the time-blocking technique supports all of these changes.

Choose one or two of your most pressing challenges to address initially. As you implement time management tech-niques, you'll see improvements in other areas. Once you achieve your milestones, switch your focus to challenges further down your list.

Set Your SMART Goal

Now that you've identified the top priority, set a SMART goal that helps you resolve it. In chapter three, you learned that SMART goals are Specific, Measurable, Achievable, Relevant, and Timely. A SMART goal is a concise sum-mary of your objective and your plan. It's crucial for your success.

Julia set a SMART goal for reducing procrastination that led her to time-blocking and all its extra benefits. I've shared it here with permission:

"I want to stop procrastinating by assigning my most important or most difficult tasks to deep work blocks and working on tasks right away if they take less than five minutes. I will assign the next day's tasks to blocks at the end of the workday and rate my procrastination on a 1 to 5 scale each day."

A few things to note about her SMART goal:

- It isn't vague. The goal and how she is going to accomplish it are clearly articulated.

- It isn't reactive. Prevention is the top priority. It's clear what steps she'll take ahead of time to reduce procrastination.

- It isn't negative. The goal is framed in a forward-looking, optimistic way.

- It isn't unrealistic. It's progressive, so she has room to make mistakes, grow from failure, and recommit. There is no pressure to be perfect.

A well-designed SMART goal doesn't mean the journey will be smooth sailing. Julia still had challenges and setbacks, but connecting to her why and setting a SMART goal made it easier for her to persevere and grow. Ultimately, Julia improved her time management because the goal she set for herself dismantled all the psychological traps that had held her back in the past.

Create a SMART goal focused on progressing in your most pressing time management challenge. Set a point in the middle and at the end of your timeline to evaluate and revise. You may find that the techniques you've chosen aren't quite right for you and need adjustment. That's okay. Learning what doesn't work is just as useful as learning what does.

Begin with One to Three

Your approach should not be about speed—even if you're in a time management crisis. I want your time management journey to be sustainable. I don't ever want a client to set off at light speed and run out of gas. I don't want that for you, either.

Your current time management behavior is a set of habits you've spent your whole life learning and reinforcing. You can't read one book and become a new person. You built your problems slowly; you'll have to dismantle them slowly. In the end, they will be corrected if you're patient and persevere. Here's how to start.

- Choose one to three techniques or practices that will drive progress on your top-priority time management challenge. One to three is a manageable number of changes for a beginner to make at one time.

- Ensure that all your changes relate to your top priority.

- Check that changes address the top priority differently and have varying levels of difficulty. The harder your techniques are, the fewer you should start with.

For example, let's say you want to reduce how much your personal life is intruding on work. There are many ways to attack this challenge: getting up an hour earlier, leaving for work or starting work 20 minutes earlier, and leaving the office or stopping work at 5 p.m. every day. These are difficult tasks that all seek to change the same habit: how you structure your time. Trying to change all three at once would be overwhelming and ultimately unsuccessful.

On the other hand, you could choose one of those difficult, time structure-related tasks and pair it with two unrelated, less difficult approaches. You could decide to leave or stop work at 5 p.m., enforce new business-hours communication boundaries with your partner, and start seeing a therapist once every two weeks. These are three efforts that would improve how your personal life impacts work. But they have various levels of difficulty and pull on different skills, habits, and parts of your lifestyle. This set of changes is much more sustainable.

Which three will you choose?

Now that your Deep Why is clear, your priority is identified, your goal is SMART, and your techniques are chosen, you have the rough contours of a plan. In the next section, we'll fill in the details to make sure you know what to do to make progress that compounds.

Create a Plan

A plan isn't just a list of techniques you intend to perform. It's a machine of moving parts that work together to get you where you want to be. You have your why and what. Keep your journal out as we explore how to figure out your how, when, and who.

In this section, we'll brainstorm a menu of regular practices from which to choose so no matter what the day brings, there's always something you can do to move forward. We'll break your ultimate goal into smaller milestones that require you to push yourself but aren't too far out of reach. Lastly, we'll identify the people most likely to help you on your journey, so you feel supported and accountable.

From Techniques to Practices

Every day is different. On some days, it will be easy to work toward your goals. On others, it will feel impossible. This is normal. Even I, a life coach who specializes in helping people become more productive, have days when my chosen practices feel too hard to do. This is why it's so important to turn your techniques into a menu of practices.

It's hard to cope with the chaos of life when you narrowly define success or chart your path to it rigidly. One bad day will make you feel like a failure and put you at risk of giving up, even if the complication isn't your fault. A menu of practices gives your method flexibility. It allows you to do more on good days and less on bad days without losing momentum. When your menu is well designed, you'll always have something you can do, even on your worst day.

So what should be on your menu? It depends on your goal. What do your chosen techniques look like under ideal circumstances? Are there any pared-back versions of those techniques that take fewer resources—even if they don't drive results as strongly? As you generate this list, keep the objective in mind: This is about having a version of your technique for every circumstance, not about finding shortcuts.

Chelsea from chapter one, who struggles with juggling her deadlines, might choose the technique of prepping for the next day before leaving for work. Ideally, that would include:

- Stopping work 30 minutes before the end of the day to prep

- Reprioritizing and rescheduling any tasks that didn't get finished

- Checking the next day's meetings

- Scheduling the next day's tasks to specific times on her calendar

- Preparing her workstation for the first task of the day

This technique sets her up for a productive day. But she's not going to have 30 minutes every day for this. What if she only has 15, or five, or one? If she has a menu that covers these scenarios, there's never an excuse not to do something to prepare for the next day.

If she only has 15 minutes, she might skip preparing her workstation and scheduling the next day's task. What if the day has been an absolute whirlwind and she only has a minute to spare? Under the worst circumstances, it doesn't take more than a minute to choose the next day's most important task, write it on a sticky note, and leave the reminder on her keyboard.

Consider the time management techniques you've chosen to start with. Are there versions of those techniques that are easier or require fewer resources? Write down as many versions as you can think of. Keep your menu handy and refer to it when circumstances are challenging. With practice, scaling your technique to fit your circumstances will come naturally.

From Practices to Milestones

Your menu of practices will make sure you're always building momentum. But momentum toward what? If your goal is ambitious, it will take time to achieve. Even with momentum, you can still run out of patience.

It's a long drive from New York City straight to Los Angeles—more than 40 hours. The 1981 blockbuster film *The Cannonball Run* made it seem full of fun and hijinks, but it would be miserable for most of us. Pittsburgh is on the way to LA, and it's only six hours away by car from NYC. Wouldn't it make more sense to have that be the first destination?

Your time management journey will be just as intense as a 40-hour cross-country drive. But if you break your goal into milestones, you can rack up wins. It's easier to keep pushing yourself if there's always a goal in sight—even if it's not the final one.

Chelsea's goal to consistently submit error-free deliverables on time will require large-scale changes to how she works. But if she breaks it into milestones that build on each other, she'll always feel like she's making progress. Her milestone map might look like this:

Starting state: Late to meetings, missing deadlines, work product has errors

Milestone 1: Consistently keep tasks and time organized

Milestone 2: Submit all deliverables on time

Milestone 3: Submit all deliverables without errors

Final milestone: Consistently submit error-free deliverables on time

Setting these milestones doesn't restrict Chelsea's ability to progress on her other time management concerns. It just focuses her efforts and keeps her optimistic and motivated. In the beginning, she will only focus on staying organized. But those efforts will naturally reduce how often she's late.

As her organization skills grow, she'll notice what seems to get in the way of submitting work on time. Once she hits that first milestone, she'll be well-positioned to begin working on the next one. While striving to turn in her work on time, she'll uncover clues as to why she makes errors, again setting her up for success in the next milestone.

What's your equivalent of stopping in Pittsburgh? Your milestones should be challenging enough that you have to work to get to them, but also be within sight of each other. They should build on one another. Achieving one should make achieving the next easier until you reach your final milestone and your goal is complete.

Tip: Assemble Your Support Team

Even if you don't work on a team, you don't work in a vacuum. What you do at work and how you do it affects people.

Who should be on your support team?

- Your boss or teammates
- Passive work bystanders (e.g., someone in another department)
- Friends and family. They know you best. They may be able to encourage you or challenge you in ways your colleagues can't.
- Professional help. Coaches like myself can provide additional structure, ideas, and accountability.
- Online support. Follow blogs, social media accounts, and online communities dedicated to time management. Check out some of my favorites at betterwithphoebe.com/inspo.

How do you assemble your support team?

- Talk to people in your organization about your desire to improve your time management.
- Tell them about your plans and ask them for support, ideas, and encouragement.
- Don't avoid asking for help.

How do you overcome fear about admitting your problem?

For women: My female clients often don't ask for help out of fear of being an inconvenience. Fight the urge to "not be a bother." Give people the opportunity to help you. The worst thing that could happen is that they say no. In that case, you've learned something important about that relationship.

For men: My male clients often don't ask for help out of fear of being embarrassed or showing weakness. Asking for help is not a sign of weakness. It's a sign of conscientiousness and dedication. It's also an opportunity to strengthen your relationship with the person whose assistance you need.

What's the payoff?

Remember Chelsea and her proofreading partner, Jesse? She was worried about being a nuisance but took the plunge and asked for help. She found that Jesse also needed proofreading support. Chelsea acquired an ally for herself and got to become an ally for her teammate.

Go for It

Don't wait any longer. Decide right now that you are committing to your time management transformation, not just for the short term, but for good. You may have felt stuck, overwhelmed, or anxious before. Decide that you're done with that. You may have been disappointed in yourself and frustrated at your untapped potential before. Decide that you're done with that.

You may have procrastinated yourself into crisis after crisis. You may have let distraction steal entire days. You may have eroded your reputation with some of your colleagues. When you add up all the time, you may have wasted years on tasks that didn't matter and techniques that didn't work.

Decide—right now—that you're done with all of that. You can do work you're proud of without living under time pressure. You can improve your productivity and reach your goals. You have all the tools. You have all the strategies. You've designed your plan. It's time to start your journey in earnest. You can be a Time Master. All you have to do is start and not give up.

The Power of Mindfulness

Use mindfulness to get you through the rough spots along the way. A person with time management issues is no stranger to anxiety and pressure. When these emotions are too intense, they reduce performance and cost time. These three practices will help you calm down when you're feeling pressure on your time management journey.

○ 3 x 3 breathing: Deep breathing reduces stress hormone levels. Try breathing in through the nose, holding the breath in, releasing through the mouth, then holding the emptiness. Stay at each stage for three counts. Repeat three times.

○ Grounding exercises: Put yourself fully in the present by taking 30 seconds to scan your environment with your senses. Notice the details around you and mentally describe them in complete sentences.

○ Gratitude: Focusing too much on what we wish was different can make us unhappy. Take a few moments each day to be grateful for what's good. If you're at a loss, remember that being alive is worth being thankful for.

Make It Sustainable

The rest of this book is dedicated to helping you not give up. You'll experience victories and setbacks as you put your plan into action. As long as you don't give up, you'll make all the improvements you hope for. But how can you push through the difficult beginning and hit your stride in the middle, so you can triumph at the end? It's all about your mindset.

Throughout this book, I've called your time management transformation "a journey." Think of your plan as the route and your techniques as the vehicle. Your mindset is the fuel. It's much easier to get started, keep going, and bounce back when your mindset is healthy and productive.

In this section, we'll explore three key skills that will keep you from quitting so you can achieve your time management goals.

Cultivate Motivation

"How can I stay motivated?" is the most common question my coaching clients ask me. It's an understandable but misguided question. Motivation is a feeling, and emotions will come and go with no regard to how much we try to control them. We can only experience and respond to them.

You can't turn on motivation any more than you can turn on happiness or turn off sadness. But when someone asks how they can stay motivated, that's precisely what they're hoping to do. This is the motivation fallacy. Motivation cannot be manufactured, but it can be cultivated.

You can design your context to make spontaneous motivation more likely. Ways to do this are peppered throughout this book, but let's review them.

- Stay connected to your Deep Why so your efforts feel meaningful.

- Set SMART goals so you have clarity about what you're trying to achieve.

- Surround yourself with people and media that encourage and help you.

- Avoid people and media that discourage you or hold you back.

While these efforts increase the likelihood of spontaneous motivation, they won't guarantee it. What do you do when it doesn't come?

A 2019 study by researchers at the University of Tennessee at Knoxville and Texas A&M found that the simple act of smiling can make you feel happier. Similarly, the simple act of starting can make you feel motivated. Once you start, it's easier to keep going. Just like smiling makes you happier, starting makes you more motivated.

Starting a task without motivation requires willpower. The more challenging or unpleasant your tasks are, the more willpower will be required. Willpower is a finite resource. It draws on your mental energy stores, just like any other thinking task. If you have to use too much will-power to get through the day, you'll feel exhausted and ultimately fail to get things done. Fortunately, willpower depletion is preventable.

When starting feels difficult and you feel yourself pro-crastinating, try to identify where the friction is coming from and remove it. I call this "clearing the runway." Over time, you'll start to notice patterns in what kind of friction you experience and what types of steps help.

Five ideas for clearing the runway:

1. Make your choices intentional. Procrastination is usually a passive choice. Observe your thoughts and feelings. Name them, state how you want them to influence you, and then make an inten-tional choice to start.

2. Break big projects into smaller, easier tasks. This helps you reframe a task so it's less intimidating. Identify one small step you can take to progress on the task and commit to doing only that.

3. Take five. Commit to working on the task for just five minutes. If you want to stop after the five minutes is over, give yourself permission to. Most likely, you'll want to keep going.

4. Reverse your focus. Don't focus on the comfort of procrastination or the discomfort of the action you're avoiding. Think about the drawbacks of procrastination and the benefits of the action.

5. Clear away clutter. Mess and clutter make our brains work harder to understand our environment's implications. When there are too many inputs, we start to feel overwhelmed or tired. Set a timer and see how much you can tidy up in 10 minutes, then start your task.

Embrace Resilience

Setbacks are inevitable. The question isn't whether or when they'll happen. The question is whether you'll allow them to make you give up on your goal. It might seem pessimistic to accept that setbacks are sure to happen. But this enables you to take a proactive approach to building resilience. Resilience helps you adapt to stress, change, and failure. In my experience, the most resilient clients excel in maintaining two attitudes: growth mindset and beginner's mind. Let's explore why each is important and how to develop them.

Growth Mindset

Growth mindset is a concept pioneered by psychologist Carol Dweck. When studying children learning, she found that some took failure in stride while others became distraught and gave up. The difference between the children who persevered and the children who gave up was what they believed about themselves.

The resilient children believed they could improve and that practice made them better. They felt confident that their capabilities could grow. The children who gave up believed that no matter how hard they worked, they'd never improve. They believe their capabilities were fixed.

If you have a fixed mindset about your time management, you'll blame setbacks on who you are and what you're capable of as a person. If you have a growth mindset, you'll view setbacks as just another step on the path to mastery. Choose to believe you can grow in your time management skills with practice, especially when you fail.

Beginner's Mind

Shoshin is a core concept of Zen Buddhism. It translates to "beginner's mind." Shoshin involves choosing to hold the perspective that there is always more to learn, no matter how much you know. It encourages you to approach learning with openness. It asks you to look for and question assumptions and preconceptions about what you're practicing to avoid cutting off new avenues of learning.

This willingness to question doesn't come from a place of skepticism, but from a place of curiosity. Under the best circumstances, beginner's mind makes learning more fun. In the face of failure, beginner's mind helps you have compassion for yourself. It allows you to view the failure from a distance, frame setbacks as opportunities to learn, and explore why it happened without placing blame.

Get Gritty

Grit is your ability to persevere in the service of long-term goals—especially if reaching them requires overcoming adversity. Growth mindset and beginner's mind help you build grit. What can you do to develop these thinking habits?

Seek encouragement from your allies.
Identify one or two cheerleaders you trust and make sure they know what you're trying to achieve. Allow yourself to be vulnerable with them and share when you're struggling. These trusted friends can provide encouragement, ideas, and accountability.

Keep your self-talk constructive.
It's okay to reflect on areas to improve, but never to mistreat yourself. You are not your mistakes. It's okay to feel bad about a setback, but don't allow yourself to wallow in regret. Negative self-talk is the enemy of a growth mindset. When you're feeling down, reflect on the hardships you've overcome in the past. Treat those experiences as evidence that you can bounce back.

Realize Your Potential

Work is a core part of our identity. Everyone wants to feel like the work they do is meaningful. That feeling—that our contributions matter—comes down to how we spend our time at work. Are you working on what matters, or are you spinning your wheels? Is the way you're spending your time helping your company grow? Is it helping you grow?

Life is an exercise in time management because time is the most precious resource you have. You don't know how much you have, but you know you'll never get more of it. Your mission should be to spend it wisely. To spend it making an impact. To spend it becoming the person you want to be. To spend it fulfilling your potential.

You may look back at how you've spent your time so far with regret. You may point to moments where you feel you could have done better, made different choices, focused on better things, or broken bad habits. You could have done a lot of things, but none of that matters in this moment. That version of you didn't know what you know now.

You know how to deal with distractions and disruptions. You know how to set up your day. You know how to recognize what's most important at work. You know how to leverage technology to keep you organized and focused. You know how to manage your emotions so you don't abandon your goals. You know how to deal with the unexpected.

When you opened this book for the first time, you had an idea of what work felt like: disorganized, anxious, and overwhelming. As you learned about time management strategies, you saw glimpses of what work could feel like: smooth, clear, and focused. You imagined, even if it was just for a moment, what work would be like if you were the master of your time.

That feeling doesn't have to be imaginary. It can be real. I believe you can do it. I believe you are powerful. I believe you will achieve great things. I believe you can master your time. All you have to do is believe it, too.

Resources

Start with Why: How Great Leaders Inspire Everyone to Take Action (2011) by Simon Sinek

The 5 Second Rule: Transform your Life, Work, and Confidence with Everyday Courage (2017) by Mel Robbins

The Four Tendencies: The Indispensable Personality Profiles That Reveal How to Make Your Life Better (and Other People's Lives Better, Too) (2017) by Gretchen Rubin

The Motivation Manifesto: 9 Declarations to Claim Your Personal Power (2014) by Brendon Burchard

*The Subtle Art of Not Giving a F*ck: A Counterintuitive Approach to Living a Good Life* (2016) by Mark Manson

References

Evans, G. W., and D. Johnson. "Stress and Open-Office Noise." *Journal of Applied Psychology* 85, no. 5 (October 2000): 779–783. doi.org/10.1037/0021-9010.85.5.779.

Fiebelkorn, Ian C., Mark A. Pinsk, and Sabine Kastner. "A Dynamic Interplay within the Frontoparietal Network Underlies Rhythmic Spatial Attention." *Neuron* 99, no. 4 (August 22, 2018): 842–853. doi.org/10.1016/j.neuron.2018.07.038.

Leather, Phil, Diane Beale, and Lucy Sullivan. "Noise, Psychosocial Stress and Their Interaction in the Workplace." *Journal of Environmental Psychology* 23, no. 2 (June 2003): 213–222. doi.org/10.1016/S0272-4944(02)00082-8.

University of Tennessee at Knoxville. "Psychologists Find Smiling Really Can Make People Happier." *ScienceDaily*. Published April 12, 2019. ScienceDaily.com/releases/2019/04/190412094728.htm.

Index

Acknowledgments

First, I have to thank my partner, Tim Greenwood. I wrote this book while working full-time, running my coaching business, moving, and filming a documentary with Netflix. He held it all together while I rode the literary emotional roller coaster. Without him, I don't know where I'd be. Certainly not putting the finishing touches on this book.

I'd have nothing to write about if it weren't for my mom, Jean Gavin. She never stopped encouraging me as I went from being a frantic, ADHD mess of a kid to my current polished, organized professional self. She has been a relentless cheerleader, and her belief in me made all the difference.

I'm not sure if I should thank my dogs, Pterodactyl and Pandora, as they were mostly a distraction. However, they do seem to be experts in time management. Each day they remind me that walks, sleep, and treats make for a happy life.

My editor, Carolyn Abate, has been a treasure. Her flexibility, humor, and experience made everything about this process easier and more fulfilling.

Lastly, I must thank every single one of my coaching clients. You are my joy and my purpose. I am endlessly inspired by your belief in yourselves, the hunger you bring to our work, the audacious goals you set, and the adversity you overcome to succeed.

About the Author

 Phoebe Gavin is a life and career coach. She helps people design lives they are proud of and excited to live using her life design program, the North Star Method. This method borrows from multiple disciplines, including design, psychology, neuroscience, cognitive science, and behavioral economics to help people set courageous goals and build sustainable systems for meeting them. She lives in Alexandria, Virginia, with her partner, Tim, and her dogs, Pterodactyl and Pandora. Learn more about her services at betterwithphoebe.com.

CPSIA information can be obtained
at www.ICGtesting.com
Printed in the USA
LVHW070428120221
679128LV00019B/1373

9 781648 760143